Plot Snakes and
the Dynamics of Narrative Experience

Plot Snakes and the Dynamics of Narrative Experience

ALLEN TILLEY

UNIVERSITY PRESS OF FLORIDA

Gainesville / Tallahassee / Tampa / Boca Raton
Pensacola / Orlando / Miami / Jacksonville

Library of Congress Cataloging-in-Publication Data appear on the last printed page of the book.

The University Press of Florida is the scholarly publishing agency of the State University System of Florida, comprised of Florida A & M University, Florida Atlantic University, Florida International University, Florida State University, University of Central Florida, University of Florida, University of North Florida, University of South Florida, and University of West Florida.

University Press of Florida
15 Northwest 15th Street
Gainesville, FL 32611

Contents

Illustrations

Preface

IN 1973 I JOINED the English faculty of the University of North Florida. We were a new upper division and graduate institution. Because we had no freshman or sophomore courses, we faced the problem of offering general education courses in the upper division. Willard Ash, dean of the College of Arts and Sciences, devised the idea of the Venture course to fill this need. Venture courses were to be interdisciplinary, experimental, and substantial.

I offered a Venture course called "Fantasy, Freud, and Science Fiction" to a class of seventy students. The course combined Sigmund Freud's *Interpretation of Dreams*, Carl Jung's *Memories, Dreams, Reflections*, a selection of novels, and *The Odyssey*. I planned the course with faith that by the end of the quarter the psychology would begin to illuminate the literature and that things would generally come together. About two weeks from the end of the course not much had. Panicked, I made plot summaries of the literature to see if I could find any resemblances that would enable me to bring some sort of closure to the course. Twenty minutes before a class I discovered that all the literary works followed a sequence of six stages. The students helped me name the stages.

Some time later I realized that all the literary works I had chosen were romances as defined by Northrop Frye in *Anatomy of Criticism* (1969). (Even later I saw ways, suggested in this book, that I might have better integrated the psychology and the literature.) Would the six-stage plot scheme work for other romances? Could I develop plot schemes for works in Frye's other modes as well? Many courses exploring these questions followed, and I took my developing ideas to around twenty scholarly meetings over the ensuing years.

Early on I saw that my work might help alleviate a problem some of my students were having with their literature courses. As one bright student told me before she dropped out of school, she felt as if she were carrying around a basket into which the literature faculty tossed books. Books were sliding off the top and out the bottom, but nothing was making collective sense.

I am aware that most scholars working on narrative would congratulate my student on discerning the true nature of literary study. Many worthy theorists are missing from my bibliography because they have nothing to add to my project, which tries to define fundamental regularities in my student's basket.

In 1976 I attended a seminar on narrative sponsored by the National Endowment for the Humanities at Yale University with Peter Brooks. Brooks was then working with the idea that plots could be treated dynamically, that a plot binds energy loosed at the beginning. Examining what I had been doing in the light of his ideas, I realized two things that excited me. The first was that all the plot schemes I had developed were systematically related through the types of energies that drive plots (until then I had separate, unrelated descriptions only). The other was that every psychology I know that describes states of mind is deeply related to narrative through the energies that psychological theorists presuppose in their conceptions of psychodynamics. Since then I have come to understand that the dominant causal system of a work determines the nature of its plot process, its dynamics. An analysis of causal modality—how meaning emerges in a narrative universe—illuminates all those narratives that share that universe and describes their fundamental similarities.

To indicate the range of narratives that share those common universes (and they *are* multiple universes) I have chosen my examples broadly. I will be discussing fictive and nonfictive narratives from a number of fields. Along with novels and short stories I include drama, film, and television situation comedy, as well as case histories, a social movement, and evolutionary theories. I have often returned to Shakespeare throughout the book in honor of his variety and of his centrality to our tradition.

I believe that I have stumbled upon an organization in the ways we make narrative sense of the world—a great coherence in the universe of narrative. I hope to record an advance in our consciousness of the stories we tell and thereby to influence the way narrative literature is understood and taught. I also hope to suggest a way of articulating concerns common to literature and to other narrative disciplines—psychology, history, sociology, and philosophy—that depend at least in part on narratization.

Portions of this book have appeared in *College English* and the *Psychocultural Review*. Richard Brautigan's "The Scarlatti Tilt" is reprinted by permission.

The ideas of other people are everywhere in this book. Sometimes I can acknowledge these people, but more often, especially in the case of my students, they have said things now lost that showed me the way I needed to go. I will at least thank Pamela Selton, who juxtaposed the news item and the Brautigan story I use in chapter 7 and who, along with others in the seminar we shared, first helped me work out ways of describing narratives that have multiple plot lines.

This long project has tested the patience of family and of colleagues. Richard Bizot, Cherrill Heaton, Nancy Levine, Michael Miller, William Slaughter, and Richard Sugg have all read stages of the manuscript and have offered helpful advice. Andrew Farkas, Peggy Pruett, and other staff at the University of North Florida Library have supported me in every way open to them. Colleagues and authorities at UNF have treated this project with what amounts to institutional magnanimity. Finally, my wife, Peggy, has encouraged and supported me throughout the years.

1

The Plot Snake

General Plot Form

THE PROJECT of determining generalizable plot shape has teased us so mercilessly that we have decided not to play any longer. In 1970 Roland Barthes predicated *S/Z* on the idea that, since literary works are so various, a critical apparatus for describing plot should be designed for one work only. His decision marked something of a milestone in a long game that began with Aristotle's *Poetics* and was continuing in the form of literary structuralism at the time of Barthes's project. Barthes announced that the game was fraudulent, a cheat. We had not found the underlying order of plot because there was none.

In 1984 our receptivity to variation had progressed to the point that Paul Ricoeur in the second volume of *Time and Narrative* contested "the very principle of *order* that is the root of the idea of plot. What is in question today is the very idea of a relationship between an individual work and every received paradigm" (7).

Hayden White in a chapter contributed to *The Future of Literary Theory* speaks for a consensus of theoreticians when he says that a general logic or even a general grammar of narrative has not been found because "the turns of any given nonformalized discourse and the order of their occurrence are not predictable in advance of their actualization in a specific utterance" (R. Cohen 1989, 28). This position is so commonly held as not to require a demonstration. Of course, to say that narrative turns (that is, changes that are meaningful in some model of narrative) have not been predicted is quite a different thing from saying that they cannot be predicted.

What follows in this book is a series of moves in the old Aristotelian game. No one ever *proved* that the game was bogus, after all. To prove irregularity in narrative, as opposed to demonstrating its presence in any given narrative, is not only impossible but the project flies in the face of our sense of some underlying dimension of familiarity in the narratives we experience.

But things have progressed so far that for the purposes of this book I need a naive reader—willfully naive, as may be—someone who will suspend the convictions expressed above. Finally, when the necessary suspension has been dissolved, by the end of the presentation a place will have been found for the valid objections of those who opt out of the game or who will critique destructively any rules whatsoever. They too have their claim on a reality.

Plot is an orderly process of change experienced by a reader who moves through a text. That experience will be conditioned by the reader's concept of the author or of the origin of the text and by a posited world of experience in which the reader can share.

"Cinderella" is a widely known and ancient story—or set of stories. Charles Perrault's seventeenth-century Cinderella of the glass slipper, Jacob and Wilhelm Grimm's eighteenth-century Aschenputtel, and Walt Disney's twentieth-century film ingenue with the fairy godmother can be said to be heroines of the same story by virtue of the general plot they share, that of tale type 510A in the Aarne-Thompson system of folktale classification (Aarne 1961). The plot of type 510A might be described by the plot snake in figure 1. So may any plot that comes to a firm conclusion.

The plot of "Cinderella" must remedy the undervaluation of the heroine after her mother's death. Following a series of events in which forces contend to keep Cinderella from or to conduct her to a public celebration, she is enormously valued in the temporary binding of the plot as the Prince chooses her from among all others and pursues her unsuccessfully. But the binding is temporary—she still appears untidy and worthless most of the time, and the Prince values her anonymously. No one really knows who she is, either from her appearance or by her inner identity, whether in rags or in finery.

The infernal vision, the maximum of disorder in the plot, includes the prospect that someone else will assume Cinderella's proper value and wear her slipper, marrying the Prince. All the worth that has been created for her may be so slippery that it slides to another person. But in the final binding only Cinderella fits her destiny, and she enters married life. The sixth stage of the plot establishes a stable world that will continue beyond the end of the story—in the Grimms' version, the stepsisters' eyes are pecked out by doves, so that their inner deformity gains an outward sign to match the new outward signs of Cinderella's beauty and election. In the

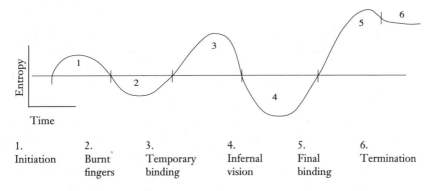

FIGURE 1. Plot Snake with General Plot Stages

ninth-century Chinese version, the termination is marked by burying the bones of a magic fish at the seashore, and the wicked stepmother and step-sister are killed by "flying stones" (Dundes 1983, 77). Perrault records that Cinderella married off the two repentant stepsisters to lords of her court.

The three endings, on the level of generality appropriate to a descrip-tion of the Aarne-Thompson tale type 510A, all establish Cinderella as royal bride and reward her stepsisters in some fitting and satisfying way. Another level of generality might distinguish the plots of the European versions from the Chinese, and, at the lowest level, identify those features that distinguished a particular reader's experience of a particular tale on one occasion. Conversely, the tale type could be so described as to relate it to many other types of tale. The general plot form is at the highest level of generality; it describes any full plot that comes to closure.

Aristotle said that a plot is like a knot. In the first part of the work, the knot is tied. At the center of the work, the knot is complete. Thereafter through the last half of the work the knot will be untied. Gustav Freytag, a German theorist of the nineteenth century, summed up the Aristotelian tradition of plot analysis by saying that a typical plot is like a pyramid: a rising action leading to a climax at the apex, and then a falling action leading to a denouement at the end. *Denouement* is from the French word for "an unraveling." What is unraveling is Aristotle's plot knot.

In a traditional plot analysis (Freytag's pyramid), our experience of the plot is said to rise to the climax and to fall from that point toward the end. Yet that description will not answer well to most people's experience of the plot of "Cinderella." In fact, it does not answer very well to the experience of anything more complex than a brief anecdote—or of an incident, perhaps forming part of an entire plot. That is why Freytag's pyramid has been such a blunt instrument for the analysis of plots. I would like to call a narrative or partial narrative that is best described by Freytag's pyramid an *episode*.

What might Freytag have meant by "rising action"? What rises? Perhaps it answers experience better to say that the movement toward the Prince's public celebration takes place in stages of successive rises and falls. In the opening of the story the danger emerges. Cinderella deals with it, first successfully, and then unsuccessfully. She finds herself unable to complete the tasks set her and gets magic help. The helper who supplies her beautiful clothes and completes her tasks may be felt as moving her up from isolation and despair.

Since a plot is a process of change, dynamic metaphors come naturally to someone trying to describe one. Something in the narrative world changes meaningfully in the course of the reader's experience, or the narrative would be static and would lack plot. The forces that cause the change may be said to drive the plot as energy may be said to drive changes in any dynamic system, and the stages of plot may be defined in terms of energy states.

Peter Brooks in *Reading for the Plot* (1984) uses Freud's *Beyond the Pleasure Principle* to develop the idea that a plot process binds some intrusive element much as repeated nightmares serve to bind the anxiety of a neurosis of traumatic onset. (One such neurosis is the type of poststress syndrome called war neurosis.) The energy that drives plot binds some disruptive intrusion, some agent of change. Otherwise the plot will lack closure.

Of course, many plots *do* lack closure, and most lack closure to some degree. A plot achieves closure to the extent that it binds the energies that drive it.

This metaphorical *binding* might be carried out in a great number of ways. When we are able to face and interact with a threatening figure in a nightmare, our fear is bound by being attached to a specific figure whom we can begin to understand and confront. Similarly, the energies of plot might be bound by being attached to some central image or family of images. In another binding strategy, some narratives (such as *Oedipus the King*) achieve a binding of energies when central truths are known and acted upon by the characters. In this case the binding is a kind of emergence. A potential for change may be bound through being annulled or through being made actual and complete. A systematic treatment of the specific binding processes of narrative must wait for the discussion of narrative modes, or kinds. Now we are concerned with the process by which a plot binds energy on the most general level of description.

Aristotle tells us that the plot of a tragedy (and, by an extension we have been making since classical commentaries on the *Poetics*, all plot) has a beginning, a middle, and an end. The middle of this plot is not hard to spot. Cinderella gets to go to the Prince's party in an appropriate dress.

The middle of a plot is the middle of *an experience*. It is not buried in a text as in the heart of a mountain, nor is it a statistical midpoint like the center of a list. If a tree falls in a text and no one watches it fall, it resonates in no plot. It just stays there falling until someone reads it. Then it becomes what it always was *in potentia*—a part of an experience, perhaps a midpoint.

Cinderella attends the party. Her success, assisted by magic animals, the soul of her dead mother, or some other agent, is the center of an experience of change. Aristotle said that plot is tied to action, and the heart of an action is change, even as plot is the soul of a work, that which makes it live. The process of change solves the problem that has driven the plot to this point—Cinderella's desire to attend the party, appropriately dressed. But the party provides only a provisional solution; it occasions a *temporary binding*. The Prince does not know who she is, and her finery disappears at the appointed time. The succeeding half of the story must provide the *final binding*, during which the fulfillment of Cinderella's desire is consistent with the other impinging conditions of her existence.

The middle of every plot that comes to any sort of satisfying conclusion is such a temporary binding. The end of every plot that has a conclusion is such a final binding. (Some narratives, such as Beckett's *Three Novels*, stop rather than conclude; others, such as most jokes, end with a disruption of the plot.)

The first actions provide the *initiation*: some novel condition is introduced into the universe of the story. In the turn of stage one, Cinderella's mother dies, and Cinderella is victimized by her new stepmother and her two stepsisters. The plot names the process by which her problems are accommodated in the world of the story. In that sense the discrepancy between Cinderella's true worth and her valuation by those around her might be said to drive the plot.

In the second stage Cinderella's victimization begins to bump things around. In this *burnt fingers* stage of plot, Cinderella turns toward the temporary binding when she is promised that she may attend the party if she performs certain impossible tasks, such as sorting good seeds from bad among those that have been cast on the hearth.

Past the *temporary binding* (the third stage, when Cinderella attends the party), the discrepancy between her true worth and her valuation reaches a maximum in the fourth, *infernal vision* stage of plot. She is both the chosen bride of the Prince and the most degraded person in her narrative world. The turn toward the *final binding* comes with her lost slipper, which provides the means by which her great natural value may be recognized by the Prince. The *termination* promises that the couple will live happily ever after.

Laurence Sterne in *Tristram Shandy* VI.40 provides a set of comically convoluted plot lines drawn to fit the plots of the volumes of his novel. (Actually, his plot line should look more like a sine wave throughout. I shall return to the topic.) With Sterne's spirit smirking somewhere behind me I have provided the plot line of figure 1. If plot is the experience of the binding of an intrusion, then some sort of representation of the fuss being kicked up by the intrusion should capture the basic shape of our experience. When the line moves up, it indicates increasing order in the narrative universe. When it moves down, it reflects growing disorder.

I do not provide a scale on the vertical dimension. That ends higher than it began because the world of the story at the opening is more unstable, less orderly, than at the end. Cinderella has reached her place in adult life at the end and is no longer susceptible to the vagaries of parental valuation. I am not sure how exact quantification of the degree of change could proceed (as opposed to the general change I indicate by the curve).

The horizontal line indicates time elapsed from the first word of the story to the last. Its location with respect to the entropy line represents a sort of baseline of order that the plot crosses as it passes from stage to stage (except for the transition from stage five to stage six).

The vertical dimension of the plot snake is entropy—the greater the entropy, the greater the disorder. (The term is borrowed from thermodynamics.) One unhandy feature of entropy for the use to which it is put here as a metaphor is that entropy grows greater as disorder increases. But experientially, a move toward order feels like a move up. So entropy increases as you move down in figure 1.

The issue is not entirely trivial. In the energy systems of thermodynamics, entropy increases with time. That is, as time goes by, any closed energy system gets more disorderly. With time, the heat in a cup of coffee placed in a closed room will disperse throughout the space. The heat will not have disappeared. Before, we knew where the heat was; now we do not. The system has become more disorderly, and entropy has increased.

Exactly the opposite happens in plots. The situation at the end of "Cinderella" is much more stable than at the beginning. The forces that would drive the fictive world of "Cinderella" into chaos have been annulled. All plots that come to a final binding enact the establishment of order.

The basic degree of order in a narrative universe varies from work to work. But I have developed no scheme to indicate entropy on either an absolute scale or on a scale relative among works. I could provide quantification along the temporal dimension by calculating the average time it takes to tell folktale 510A. The time line always represents experiential time as the reader progresses sequentially through the work. That means if we learn something in the middle of the work that happened in the distant past, it still happens *in the middle of the work* so far as our experience of the plot is concerned.

By representing the plot in this way, I mean to emphasize that the process stages are really representations of regions of change—indications of basic turns in the plot. The exact boundaries between, say, the initiation and the burnt fingers stage may be more or less blurred in any given plot. My only claims are that the stages given are the minimum number to accommodate the changes in a full plot (with the occasional exception of the termination stage), and that they are generally as I have described them. The "rising action—falling action" tradition of plot interpretation is simply inadequate to the experience of most plots. I should add that terms like *denouement, catastrophe,* and *climax* are useful only when their received usage happens to fit the kind of plot under consideration.

The sixth stage, termination, is attenuated or missing in many developed plots. I have waffled on whether it should be included among the basic stages or treated as a common but not universal subdivision of the final binding. Finally, my reason for preferring to treat it separately is that my students are more comfortable with it this way. It helps them deal with more kinds of plots more successfully to look for a termination and to treat as special cases those plots that lack the stage (as does the apocalyptic conclusion of *The Nibelungenlied*) or that represent it with a single sentence, as in Hemingway's *A Farewell to Arms:* "After a while I went out and left the hospital and walked back to the hotel in the rain."

The smallest unit of a plot was defined by Vladimir Propp as a *function,* "an act of a character, defined from the point of view of its significance for the course of the action" (1968, 21). The advance Propp's term makes over the Aristotelian term *action* is that with it he locates the action in a process, if it is to be part of the plot, while Aristotle makes an action's inclusion in the plot part of a value decision and not a definitional matter.

I would like to read Propp's "significance" of action as a necessary inclusion of the reader within M. H. Abrams's fundamental quaternity of author, story, world, and reader (in his more general terms, artist, work, universe, and audience) (1953, 6). No critical theory that excludes any of the four can be adequate. Abrams observes that most critics emphasize one or the other. He puts the work in the center. Mikhail Bakhtin as well as many contemporary reader response theorists seem to omit the world and place the reader's linguistic capacity in the center. Wayne Booth and others interested in the ethical dimension of narrative experience move the world toward the center.

I see *author, story, world,* and *reader* as four equally important terms, each detachable only at the expense of misrepresenting the narrative experience. Even when the narrative is a dream, all four attend: the dream, the dreamer as maker, the dreamer as watcher, and the world as context and referent. The parts of the dream, like the parts of any narrative, will enact a process of change arising from the creative activity of the mind, perceived by the mind, and spoken with reference to the place of that mind in space and time.

Drama is sometimes distinguished from narrative because it (like most dreams) is acted, not told. I should admit now that I do not make a *fundamental* distinction between drama and other forms of narrative, however helpful it may be in some situations to call attention to its character as performance. The author of drama is collective, as it is of film and television narrative, but the radical of presentation does not place drama in some special category as regards basic plot dynamics.

An experience of the text as a process of change is built of whatever in the text can suggest and evoke an attitude, an interest, a value, a fear, or a desire, or indeed any of the characteristics of disposition we might care to delineate by such words. But to be a part of the plot, that feature must have a past or a future in our experience of the text: it must be considered as a feature of change, and hence as a function. If the function forms a part within the primary continuity in our experience of the text, it is a part of the main plot line.

My experience as I read a text is controlled by other factors than the text. (May I use "read" as shorthand for all the ways I can experience a text, whether enacted, spoken, mimed, or imagined?) Readers bring to the event that amalgam of age, moral development, and experience of life suggested by the term *maturity*. This maturity will have been achieved in the terms afforded by readers' culture, defined by Clifford Geertz as the ordered system of meanings and symbols by which we live (1973, 144–45).

Readers will also bring to a work some degree of literary and linguistic experience. That experience may enable readers to react to a work in ways atypical of their culture and level of maturity—for example, to understand a work in a language other than a reader's native tongue, or to experience as important questions of theology no longer of interest in a reader's culture. Finally, to catch whatever factors slip through my other terms, each reader will have a particular identity that will include sexual orientation and the kinds of choices made in otherwise indifferent situations.

The constantly increasing flow of new things we find to say about old texts testifies to the changes of readerly experience with time. Within one time frame, a hypothetical Western naif (say, a six-year-old child) and an adult, culturally Chinese reader would always experience a different plot in reading the same text.

The author in a reader's experience is the constructed or implied origin of the text. The author of a given experience of a text is really constituted by a horizon of readerly expectations. The author helps determine our emotional experience, which must influence plot on some level.

Reader, world, and author all change the plot as they shift. Assuming a stable text, among the possible experiences that that text can yield, is any privileged? Is there an Ur-plot around which the others cluster?

I have taught *Beowulf* every year for about twenty years and have found it a little different each time. I could construct a normative reading only at a certain level of generality. It would have to include my sense of the reader implied by the cultural context of the tale, its world as I am able to share it.

What about a Martian reading of the Grimms' version of "Cinderella," or an uninformed Western reading of the Chinese version? There we can make a value judgment—if we assert a condition of commentary. The condition is this: the culture of origin of a text is privileged. By this principle, to read Sheh Hsien's story (she is the ninth-century Chinese Cinderella reported by R. D. Jameson in Dundes 1983, 71–97) we must try to sympathize with veneration for the bones of a pet fish and not to expect the King to be perfect even if he is appropriate for Cinderella, just as we must allow for the virulent misogyny of many medieval texts if we are not to be blinded by our values. The justifications for such an assertion are at least twofold. A text is most rich with potential when it is allowed the full context of its origins; one of the uses of literary study is to allow us to contact other minds in other times and places, and thereby be more in contact with the conditions of our historical existence. To that end, insofar as we are able, we reconstruct ourselves as readers in the culture of origin. Recovering the cultural contexts of past literature is one of the great projects of literary scholarship. In the past twenty years we have experienced a great shift in our conception of medieval culture, and our understanding of the literature of the period has shifted with our understanding of the context.

The reading of the naif, the Martian, is inferior to that of the sophisticate. We must share enough of the code to understand the utterance; this assertion is a corollary of the "privileged culture" condition.

Probably some ranges of experience become inaccessible to the jaded literary palate. I have scarcely read any later literary death with half the intensity I felt at twelve when Albert Payson Terhune allowed his main character to die in *Lad, A Dog*. But I do not mourn my diminished capacity for affect; Milan Kundera's *The Unbearable Lightness of Being* would have left me cold at twelve. I understand more and can encompass different kinds of experience. Of two readings, the one evincing a higher degree of literary and linguistic experience of the text's original culture is privileged. A reading that does not observe literary and linguistic codes is inferior to one that does. A good folklorist is a "better" reader of "Cinderella" than an eight-year-old girl (though she may be more profoundly moved and find the tale more important to her than it is to the folklorist) because the specialist will understand more of the author and world of the tale. In this view, consciousness is an absolute value.

In "The Affective Fallacy," Wimsatt and Beardsley warn that in confusing a text and the experience it affords, we end "in impressionism and relativism" and "the poem itself, as an object of specifically critical judgement, tends to disappear" (Wimsatt 1954, 21). Stanley Fish, among others, has stated his willingness to accept the theoretical disappearance (1972, 384). Of course, he continues nonetheless to enlarge my experience of texts.

When a text disappears (in other than a rhetorical or ideological sense), so does the experience it might afford. It is true that the locus of experience is not in the text, which stands between author and reader. Nor is it in the author, the horizon of origin. The position that all readings must measure themselves against the intention of the author is psychologically naive, even where a single psyche can be said to be the source of the narrative (as is not the case with, say, a sitcom episode). For the author is not composed of simple intentions but of many systems of intentions, some of them conflicting with one another. Moreover, narrative is a public act and therefore innately shared. When we cannot define language on the individual level we cannot expect a text to be so defined either. It exists in a public space, partially the creation of author and of reader.

Nor does the reader exist as some pure and autonomous site of experience. As reader, the subject is conditioned by participation in the narrative. Finally, the narrative experience rests on what Kitaro Nishida calls absolute experience. Whatever distinctions into author, text, reader, and world we make are descents from the unity of experience. We make such moves in order to have the basis for analytical observations that we could not otherwise articulate, observations that finally point to an object they cannot directly express: the absolute experience.

To make general plot form more clear, I will give some more examples from stories known to most of us.

"Hansel and Gretel" is driven by parental hostility. The children are intentionally lost in the forest at the urging of their stepmother (in the Grimms' source, their mother) because food is short. In the temporary binding, they discover a house you may eat. But it harbors a cannibalistic witch, who in the infernal vision prepares to eat Hansel with Gretel as an hors d'oeuvre. Gretel, who has done little but weep to this point, tricks and bakes the witch in the final binding. When the children return home in the termination they find their stepmother dead and their father newly loving.

What seemed to be the problem at first was to get enough to eat. After the temporary binding, though, the full nature of the plot becomes clear. Food shortages are secondary. The witch has food all around her. She just likes to eat kids.

After the temporary binding of "Cinderella" we acknowledge that it is not enough for her to wear fine clothes and get to go to parties where she is admired. She needs to take her place in the adult world as a greatly valued person.

Oedipus may believe until the temporary binding of Sophocles' *Oedipus the King* that his plot is all about finding the murderer of Laius, his father. In the infernal vision he finds what that discovery entails, and the final binding leaves Jocasta a suicide and Oedipus self-blinded with her brooches, his history open to the world. The termination sends him to wander in exile.

Dorothy discovers in the temporary binding of *The Wizard of Oz* that getting to the wizard in the Emerald City only begins the solution to her problems. Now she must face the wicked witch on her home ground. Dorothy's and Gretel's witches live in the same psychological neighborhood.

Hamlet takes decisive action in his temporary binding by killing Polonius and only succeeds in becoming a father killer himself. In the infernal vision he will struggle in Ophelia's grave with the son of the father he has murdered, having just sent his two schoolfellows off to be killed. Exactly what is bound in *Hamlet* is difficult to say. I will try, though, in a later chapter.

Luke Skywalker in the first installment of *Star Wars* believes that his problem is to rescue Princess Leia from the Death Star, just as Odysseus believes in the first half of *The Odyssey* that his problem is to return to Ithaca. Past the temporary binding, both find that their real task lies still ahead—to save the rebels from the forces of the Empire, and to rescue Ithaca and Odysseus's family from the suitors.

The Origins of Plot in the Life Cycle

The nature of the plot snake becomes clearer when it is seen in the context of its primal origin, the life cycle. Frank Kermode in *The Sense of an Ending* (1967) makes it clear that while we always live "in the middest" we give our life stories closure in the tales we tell. That is, we imagine our lives whole by a kind of habitual prolepsis.

The stages of a complete life were the same for Confucius and Plato as for us. Vague notions about life expectancy have engendered the popular idea that lives in the past were cut short with Hobbesian brevity. But a full life for as far back as we know was about what it is now, and life cannot be said to be complete until we have attained at least three score and ten years.

Along the way we all, male and female, of whatever race in whatever period, experience a common underlying rhythm. We are born. We achieve psychic autonomy to match our physical separation from our mother's body. We undergo puberty. We achieve adult status, marked, it may be, by the birth of our own children. We experience menopause, if we are women, and perhaps even if we are not—but in any case we undergo a midlife transition, as described for men in our culture by Daniel Levinson and his coauthors in *The Seasons of a Man's Life* (1978). And we all die. These five stages of life are marked by the primary biological passages of life: birth, puberty, parenthood, menopause, and death.

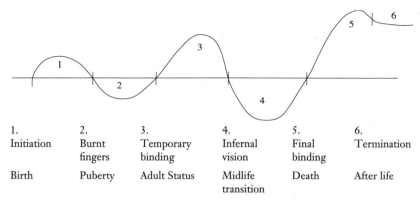

1.	2.	3.	4.	5.	6.
Initiation	Burnt fingers	Temporary binding	Infernal vision	Final binding	Termination
Birth	Puberty	Adult Status	Midlife transition	Death	After life

FIGURE 2. General Plot Form and the Life Cycle

In figure 2 I show the relationship of the plot snake to stages of the life cycle.

The six process stages of complete, nonironized plots suggest parallels with the psychobiological organization of a complete life. I recognize that the course of life can be divided in diverse ways. I wish to propose only one here, the one most closely tied to psychobiological markers.

The early years of character formation are like the initiation stage of a plot in which the concerns of a narrative emerge. The energy that drives a plot intrudes on a previously stable world much as a new life enters the world. The turn of the initiation comes with the realization that we are separate from our mothers, have our own identity.

The years of adolescence find their plot turn with the achievement of sexual maturation. Personality disorganization in puberty corresponds to the disruption and growing entropy of burnt fingers.

Life finds its temporary binding in the achievement of a mature social identity and in the acceptance by the larger world in a life role that come with the years of young adulthood, often accompanied by marriage and the birth of children.

Sometime in middle age the security offered by friends, family, and occupation dissolves at least partially in the infernal vision of the midlife crisis. One is confronted with the provisional nature of identity and of life itself.

The final binding comes in the full maturity of old age. Whatever final view of life—our own and life in general—we are to achieve, we achieve then. We are then closest to the simultaneous emergence of the great contraries. Socrates said that the task of a philosopher is to learn to die well. In that spirit, death is the final binding—the state in which we achieve a comprehensive vision.

The termination stage sees beyond the final binding to whatever continues after the individual life is over. The sixth stage of the plot concerns the relation of our life plot to the larger world. The termination may be imagined in many ways—society marching on, a heaven with harps, a merging with the *anima mundi*, annihilation, or an experience of sheer duration.

Some narratives relate more strongly to certain stages of the life plot than to others—"Cinderella" is obviously for children, and we displace ourselves somewhat in that direction to read it well. I have found that the life plot hypothesis helps me understand which works are more likely to appeal to younger students, which to older (not that younger students should be expected to have no interests beyond career and marriage). I now understand and sometimes resist my tendency to choose works most concerned with the trials of the infernal vision, my current stage.

Giambattista Vico drew an analogy between the life of civilizations and the life of an individual. The world plot implied in Revelation equally reflects the life plot sketched here; the chart of the shape of history in the *Interpreter's Bible*'s discussion of Revelation takes much the shape of my plot snake.

Most myths of history locate us in the infernal vision stage of the universal plot. The world is as chaotic, as evil as it ever gets, whether in the Hindu, the Aztec, the Germanic, or the Christian scheme of things. Perhaps that is because the people who most owned the myths, who were dominant in the societies in which the myths arose, were at that stage of their lives. They projected their stage of the life cycle onto the stories they told. Or perhaps they divined that we really are at the infernal vision, the midlife transition, of the story of our species.

Location in life resonates in our narrative experience. All narrative is the fiction of experience, and distinctions between fiction and nonfiction finally count for little, as theorists have been observing at least since Nietzsche.

To move further toward an adequate description of narrative experience it is necessary to examine the kinds of worlds it prepares us to inhabit. One modern genre that imagines a continuity of experience on the scale of the old myths of history is the theory of evolving consciousness, the subject of the next chapter.

2

Narrative Mode in Models of Evolving Consciousness

GENERAL PLOT FORM can only discern similarities among all narratives that move toward closure (and cannot deal with those that do not). The next step in a systematic approach to narrative experience must entail describing narrative kinds or modes. Starting with Abrams's quaternity we might look for kinds of readers, texts, authors, and narrative worlds.

In *The Theory of the Novel*, Georg Lukács approaches the novel in terms of the motives and situation of authors, the horizon of origin. The existential homelessness at the root of the novel arises from the author's cultural situation. Perhaps Marxist genre theory naturally gravitates to consideration of the horizon of origin. Certainly one kind of psychoanalytic criticism does so. The Marxist and author-centered psychoanalytic approaches are essentially generic theory through case history. The work illustrates a social or psychological authorial position.

The usual approach of lit 1—"In this course we will read poetry, fiction, and drama"—is based on a supposedly systematic division by textual form. Presentation (for example, as film or novel) or literary lineage determines kind. The anxiety most of us teachers of literature feel before the profusion of lyric forms is based on the unstated assumption that if we just knew all the forms we would have some effective map of lyric. Therefore our students must learn to distinguish among sonnet types. The history of textual form, influence studies, and the like have their interest and rewards but may perhaps not constitute the central determinants of generic differentiation.

To distinguish literary kind by reader is a recent enthusiasm. I have been told by a colleague in the past year that a white reader can read Alice Walker but not Toni Morrison—that is, not *really* read *Beloved*, nor have anything to say about the novel worth hearing. Can a man read anything by a woman? Can (or should) a woman read anything by a man? To what end and with what attitude should and does an Anglo read Chicano literature, or literature in translation? Do we read anything but ourselves, over and over?

These enterprises of approaching literary kind through text, author, and reader are well under way. They have not yet been successful in creating any comprehensively useful and systematic approach to literature. I feel that they are doomed to marginality and even to shallowness as systematic theories of literature, whatever rich statements they generate about their subject. Reader, author, and text all meet in the narrative world, *the site of metaphorical change*. An approach through the narrative world, at the heart of the narrative experience, will therefore develop the most profound distinctions.

Frye's Modes as Modes of Experience

Meaning arises through the association of elements. (Even a symbol derives its numinosity from the elements it gathers in its penumbra.) No feature of the narrative experience is more fundamental than meaning. The most fundamental division among narratives will be in terms of the kinds of ways meaning arises.

Simple causality underlies most of our perceptions of meaning. I strike the desk; it makes a sound. To be perceived as a cause, my blow must be contiguous in time and in space to the effect, the sound. If the sound occurs five minutes later or ten feet away I must seek other causal elements.

The cause must also precede the effect; a sound preceding the blow must have other causes.

The blow must be sufficient to the sound. If I must also lift my left foot, that must be included as a cause.

Finally, the blow must necessarily produce the sound, or I have observed a merely statistical association. (It is on this point that Hume observed that cause and effect are properties of the mind and not of events, because necessity is a matter of expectation and not of event. We can never be objectively *sure* that the next time we strike the desk it will not remain silent.)

A narrative world organized by such causal processes operating in the present is *low mimetic*. Meaning arises through human motivation, through desire and fear, as humans cause changes.

Accidental events might occur through understandable causal processes, but meaning in narrative is a property of human agency. All our stories are human stories, no matter what they seem to be about.

High mimetic narrative worlds violate the ordinary constraints on contiguity in time and space. Ancient events (events prior to any choices the present characters have made) emerge as causes of events in the present. In such primal causation, characters may find that their choices have been determined or that they have been working without knowing it to further the emergence of some primal pattern. Meaning arises not through the operation of desire and fear in the present but through the emergence of a primal determination.

Romantic narrative worlds violate the normal constraint on the priority of cause as well as the constraints on contiguity. In romance the final cause of events is the *telos*, the end or goal toward which events are proceeding. Events that seem to have no causal connection in the present are teleologically organized by the drive toward some future state. Meaning in such a narrative world arises through the willing and unwilling movements of the characters toward the telos, and through the emergence of its shape as the narrative progresses. Weak teleological causation merely entails an intention to move toward some future state. The causal modality of romance is strong teleology—the future state acts to organize events causally in the present. Often, though, events in the present threaten to defeat the teleological organization, and characters must act to bring the telos about.

In an *ironic* narrative world events relate by sheer contingency. In such a world meaningful change cannot arise. Narratives may be ironized, but cannot embody a fully ironic causation without becoming static and therefore ceasing to be narrative. Irony violates the normal causal constraint of necessity. Also, in a contingent world priority ceases to be meaningful. Past and future are impossible to distinguish without meaningful change.

The narrative world of *myth* is organized in such a way that every event is ultimately meaningful, and every event causally implies every other event. When we receive myth as myth, it violates the ordinary constraints on cause and effect by dissolving the distinction between the two. Causation is pervasive in a mythic narrative universe.

The five modes originate with Northrop Frye in *Anatomy of Criticism* (1957). He observed in his first essay that Western literary history could be described as an orderly succession: myth to romance to high mimesis to low mimesis to irony. He defined his historical modes in terms of the relative power of the characters in their worlds, from the mythic characters who are greater in kind than we to the characters of irony who seem to be baffled by the simplest tasks. Frye also observed that we have a different emotional relationship to works in the different modes.

I do not wish to represent Frye's discussion of the modes in detail because I have redefined them above and do not want to defend his definitions, which have often been attacked. Many scholars have found his modal system useful in spite of its definitional weaknesses. Even outside literature, people have applied the terminology—for example, Hayden White in history and Roy Schafer in psychology. I believe that my approach goes closer to the root of things than Frye's and that he descried an underlying order that his formulations failed to define. The upshot is that I wish to make his vocabulary work better.

Frye's system was based solely on literature, and he meant it to apply to literature only. In my redefinition, the modes characterize experience generally. We need not assume the absolute validity of the strong form of teleological causation to recognize its presence in some narratives, but we must see romance as more than a fictive mode if we are to understand the mode fully. The same goes for the other modes.

To begin to investigate the modes I propose a genre of nonfictional, nonliterary narratives: theories of evolving consciousness. I hope to demonstrate the power of the modal approach to develop a framework for meaningful comparison and commentary (and not a mere classification). The subject matter should indicate the extent to which the modes are nonliterary organizers of experience generally.

Nebuchadnezzar's Dream

The second chapter of the Book of Daniel records that Nebuchadnezzar threatened to execute all the wise men of Babylon unless one of them could recount to him and interpret the dream that the king knew he had dreamed but could not recall. Daniel and his companions were among the endangered. In answer to their prayers, the mystery was revealed to Daniel in a night vision.

The dream was of a great being with a head of gold, breast and arms of silver, belly and thighs of brass, legs of iron, and feet of mingled iron and clay. An unhewn stone destroyed the image, and the wind blew the remains away like chaff. The stone grew until it became a mountain that filled the earth. Daniel interprets the king's dream to be a vision of the succession of kingdoms from the golden present (Nebuchadnezzar is the head of gold) until the time when a rock unhewn by man shall smash a degenerate order of human history, founding in its place a kingdom that shall not pass away. (Yahweh's altar in early sections of Genesis is an unhewn stone.)

The dream has furnished our culture with a powerful figure for successive ages of civilization, ending in apocalypse. Dante remembers the dream in his *Inferno* where the composite man's tears are said to be the source of the rivers of hell. Frye's historical succession of modes is a modern parallel, with the ironic mode as companion of a culture in its endgame days.

An unusual feature of the king's dream is that in it the present is golden. In the Western tradition the Golden Age, like Eden, is usually in the inaccessible past, available to living people only as a memory (though perhaps to the fortunate dead as a state in the hereafter). Greek, Hindu, and Aztec traditions, as I have observed, all present systems of mythic historical change, ones in which the present is not golden but an extreme degeneration from the golden past. That is, they are written from the perspective of middle age. The mystery of mythic temporal location in Daniel is dispelled when we discover that it was written under the rule of Antiochus Epiphanes in the second century B.C.E, the time of mingled iron and clay, and only purports to be written four hundred years earlier in the reign of Nebuchadnezzar. In other words, the actual present of the text is the infernal vision of its plot of time. (The Revelation to John, which locates the present in the burnt fingers stage of the plot history, is a genuine anomaly.)

The Western tradition of analysis and speculation concerning historical change on a broad scale possesses no beginning, end, or middle. One may choose to pick up strands just about anywhere in antiquity: the Enuma Elish, the Babylonian creation epic with its scheme of mythic ages, which must have influenced Hebrew thought; Heraclitus, who seems to have imported Eastern schemes of change into the Western tradition; Plato, who devised a rational scheme of political transformations; late Jewish apocalyptic literature, which influenced the ensuing Christian scheme of history (the story of Nebuchadnezzar's dream is an example of Jewish apocalyptic literature); and, perhaps most nearly central of all, the Jewish conviction of election recorded in the Torah, a mission both social and divine that presupposes an orderly shape to history.

Charles Darwin certainly has added impetus to the search for an adequate conception of the order to be found in history. Since *On The Origin of Species by Means of Natural Selection* we have been presented with a problem that is new to explicit speculation. If humans, along with all else that lives on Earth, occupy a space on an evolutionary continuum that blends in its origin with the inanimate world, then the psyche must also be supposed to have an evolutionary history and future. What are the stages of its evolution? What causes change?

The group of writers I wish to consider are concerned with charting the evolution of human consciousness. They date, in one sense, only from Darwin; in another sense they extend the preexisting tradition of broad-scale historical analysis in a new direction, perhaps a tangent.

The relationship between consideration of the development of societies in history and of the evolution of consciousness may be close, for, without judging which is of prior importance, we can agree that the way we think and the way we live have much to do with one another. Still, many people since Darwin have written of the history of the psyche somewhat in isolation from consideration of the shape of social history. Among them are Teilhard de Chardin, C. G. Jung, Erich Neumann, Sigmund Freud, and Julian Jaynes.

I take the project of writing an evolutionary history of the psyche to be an interesting contemporary instance of our general drive in this culture to find a shape in history. If we can discern a broad consistency in the ways we envision our psychic past, we will have come to understand something about the ways we organize reality. We will have begun to investigate the categories in terms of which we locate ourselves in the continuum of human experience. I therefore propose to analyze some analysts of psychic evolution. Of course I must simplify their ideas; I will be content if I do not seriously distort them. I mean to emerge with a broad outline sufficiently sensitive to be of some use in locating the reader within historiography through distinctions based on causal modality.

All theories of the evolution of consciousness must distinguish among discrete historical states of the psyche: if the psyche does not change, there is nothing to analyze. All must choose realms of metaphor within whose terms the process of change is defined: one must devise a consistent map of language to chart the territory of psychic change. And all must posit a process of change that assumes that events are related in some way, causal or otherwise.

Teilhard in *The Phenomenon of Man* (1965) and elsewhere describes a vision of the great movement of evolution. Four states of matter form the framework: prelife, life, thought, and convergence to the Omega Point. Prelife is the original preconscious state of matter—that of a rock or a gas, for instance. *Consciousness*, in Teilhard's use of the term, applies to all psychisms, and thus to all life, even from the bacterial beginnings. Thought, unique to humans, is characterized by reflection: knowing that one knows.

Teilhard believed that the tendencies of psychic evolution indicated a future in which a center of all centers of thought on Earth would emerge into our awareness. He called this center the Omega Point. Early in the development of his thought he considered the Omega Point the end and goal of evolution; later he came to feel that the Omega Point was simply the most distant development he could deduce from the data and was not necessarily a terminal condition.

Teilhard uses the language of evolutionary biology as his primary metaphorical system. He is also concerned to articulate his thought in terms of Christian theology, but science, and not religion, contributes the terms with which he usually formulates the evolution of consciousness.

For Teilhard, life is a tendency of matter, and the Omega Point is the tendency of life. Radial energy tends to increase in time along any evolutionary phylum. Radial energy is what Bergson's élan vital becomes in the thought of his pupil Teilhard. It is the energy of consciousness, stemming from the center (the Omega Point) and thus radial in opposition to tangential energy, the sort we have devised the laws of thermodynamics to describe and we use to light our houses. Radial energy is free of the strictures of entropy—rather, it is negentropic, tending toward organization and structure rather than the reverse. The causal laws of thermodynamics apply less and less well to living matter as it becomes more conscious and thus more fully dependent on radial energy.

The Omega Point is at the center of evolution—and yet it is in the future. For Teilhard, we are being pulled into the future more than we are being pushed by the past. The Omega Point has been drawing us toward consciousness since time began. The dynamics of evolution for Teilhard may be called teleological. We are trying to become something. Teilhard is concerned with the conditions under which our development was possible, the sorts of considerations of climate and of material environment that we are used to seeing in treatments of evolutionary development, but he does not seek in these conditions the explanation for evolution.

Further, Teilhard's system of evolutionary causation may be called linear and unitary. A single cause, the Omega Point (or something greater, beyond speculation, that lies on the far side) is the final cause of the development of life. The Omega Point draws us through history to the time when we become it (or join it?).

Jung never undertook a systematic exploration of the entire evolutionary history of the psyche. On the other hand, few other subjects engaged him more persistently throughout his writings. He was most concerned with the forms of the emergence and consolidation of the individual consciousness, of the drive toward wholeness that he calls individuation. Individuation, the "evolution" of the individual, follows the general pattern of the development of the psyche as a whole. Jung often discussed special features of the development of consciousness (especially in *Aion*, which is about the development of Western consciousness) and inspired others to treat the subject.

Jung's primary and constant distinction is between the conscious and the unconscious mind. Jung's conception of the development of consciousness in the individual may be divided into stages. Because for Jung the history of the development of consciousness is repeated in broad outlines in the development of every individual consciousness ("ontogeny recapitulates phylogeny," as Ernst Haeckel's biogenetic law is often summarized), these stages of individual development may be taken to apply in their broad outlines to the development of consciousness in general.

Using the plot snake, the plot of Jungian individuation may be schematized as follows. Initiation: a call to individuation comes to the developing individual from the unconscious, typically in a dream or in some disruption of normal activities—perhaps through a neurosis. Burnt fingers: the person becomes aware of powerfully activated archetypes that draw their energy from the resources of the unconscious and force themselves on the person's awareness. Temporary binding: gradually a transcendent function forms, a vantage point from which the individual can integrate the primary forces of the submerged self. Infernal vision: however, the energy flowing from the unconscious inappropriately inflates the conscious self, creating what Jung calls the mana-personality (from the Polynesian word for psychic power). In the final binding of individuation the person centers on an archetype of wholeness in the unconscious, reestablishing a proper balance of energy among conscious and unconscious parts of the self. The sixth stage, termination, is the return to the business of life. I find this process most systematically described in the second of Jung's *Two Essays on Analytical Psychology*, although I believe it to be consistent with his work from *Symbols of Transformation* on. The process describes the kind of Jungian analysis that comes to closure. A more detailed look at romance would be necessary to go further with the plot of Jungian analysis.

Jung's most pervasive system of metaphor is drawn from myth, if that term may be stretched to include the imagery and concepts of such fields as alchemy and astrology. To be sure, he uses the vocabulary of psychoanalysis and extends it with his own terms—*persona*, *archetype*, and *intro-*

vert among them. But the process of individuation that Jung found in his own experience and in that of patients is recorded in myth, alchemy, and the history of religion. Indeed, myth furnishes the language in which the process occurs. In this sense it furnishes Jung's primary metaphorical system. When in *Aion* he discusses the evolution of Western consciousness it is in terms of astrology and Christian myth. Myth is the language of the unconscious, and Jung's great project is to understand what that language is telling us.

Properly, then, Erich Neumann's *The Origin and History of Consciousness* (1954), to which Jung gives approval in his preface, is couched in mythic terms. The hero emerges from an Uroboric unity (after the Uroboros, an ancient figure of the universe as a snake with its tail in its mouth), consolidates his identity through a slaying of the father and the mother, and finally achieves a higher unity of self symbolized in the myth of Osiris, whose scattered members are united and brought back to life. (Neumann's theory is male-centered. Jung, on the other hand, usually accommodated gender distinctions.)

For Neumann, as for Jung, ontogeny of psychic development is taken to recapitulate phylogeny to the extent that historical development of the psyche follows this scheme as well. The history of the emergence of the psyche may be satisfactorily observed in the process of individuation. The necessary prior condition of individuation—that is, the historical development of the archetypes—is a precondition of the development of the psyche in general. The archetypes are formal tendencies of consciousness, our tendency to experience the world in a certain way. One of Jung's favorite examples of the emergence of an archetype was the experience of falling in love. The experience is both typical and compelling, almost as if one were possessed. Neither Jung nor Neumann is much concerned to speculate on the conditions under which the archetypes developed or on the state of the psyche in intermediate stages of archetype development.

The impulse to individuation comes from the future, from something the person is called to become. While it would betray Jung to speak in terms of strictly causal systems, the meaningful pattern of change through which a person moves in integrating the self is directed toward a goal of wholeness and is in this sense teleological. The impulse to become psychically whole acts to alter the dynamic balance between conscious and unconscious factors and expresses itself synchronically (that is, through meaningful coincidences) as well as causally. External reality cooperates in moving the person toward the goal of wholeness; little and large "accidents" point the way. For Jung, events in the world are richly organized and personally referential. In a general way the statement applies to Teilhard as well. It does not apply at all to Sigmund Freud. When we turn to his works from those of Teilhard and the Jungians, we have the feeling of entering a different universe.

Freud speaks of the development of the human mind in two ways. The first is biological. The ego develops around the id in a way analogous to or identical with the development of the cortical layer of the brain (see *Beyond the Pleasure Principle*, 24; *Moses and Monotheism*, 96; and lecture 31 of *New Introductory Lectures;* all citations of Freud are to *The Standard Edition*, 1953–74). This line of thinking, scarcely developed in his published work, is a remnant of Freud's early interest in developing a physical model of the mind, as extensively documented in Frank J. Sulloway's *Freud, Biologist of the Mind* (1979).

Far more frequent are Freud's discussions of the ideas first advanced in *Totem and Taboo*. In this model, the primal horde of brothers murders and eats the father, who has forbidden them sexual access to the women of the group (their mothers and sisters). The event is imagined to have occurred in every human community, again and again, over a period of thousands of years. In *Moses and Monotheism* Freud came to the position, only hinted in earlier works, that the incident is preserved in archaic memory traces.

From the original patricide arise both guilt and the repression of instinct, for the murderous brothers willingly cede sexual control of the mothers and sisters to one of their number, probably the youngest brother, establishing repression and civilization at a stroke. From this original repression of instinct arises the modern mind with all its civilized constructs. In *Civilization and Its Discontents* Freud speculates on the primal conditions under which specific cultural forms developed.

Freud's basic distinction in psychic history is between pre-Oedipal humans (before patricide had become part of our mental furniture) and Oedipal humans. His metaphorical universe is the family and its relationships; these furnish the basic terms by which the change occurs. His causal system, firmly determinist, is primal. The human mind is the product of primal guilt. Causally, the biological and anthropological arguments are identical. In both we are captives of original structure. Freud envisions no further development. For him, the past is all.

For Julian Jaynes the present plays the role of the past in Freud and of the future in Jung. With Jaynes we are in yet another universe. His *The Origin of Consciousness in the Breakdown of the Bicameral Mind* (1976) turns on the distinction between the conscious and the unconscious mind. By consciousness Jaynes means an analog of reality, built from language, that displays the features of spatialization, excerption, an analog "I," a metaphorical "me," narratization, and conciliation. Consciousness, according to Jaynes, is as recent as the second millennium B.C.E. Indeed, it did not develop in China until Confucius and comes to South America only with the conquistadores. Consciousness develops first in the West, but in a text as late as the *Iliad*, Jaynes finds no subjective consciousness, no ego. The stages in the development toward consciousness are linguistic.

The period 1300–800 B.C.E. is crucial to the development of consciousness, for at this time the bicameral mind broke down. (Jaynes is thinking of the left brain–right brain split, which he imagines as an original unity.) While the causes of consciousness are multiple, Jaynes cites two as primary. The imperial and commercial expansion of Assyria exerted great pressure on the populations of previously undisturbed city-states. The old bicameral mind was unable to engender or deal with the levels of deception natural to the growing volume of trade. Too, the volcanic eruption of Thera about 1500 B.C.E. led to social friction occasioned by the large groups of wandering refugees. A period of great misery and violence ensued until humankind had adjusted to its new mentation. Indeed, we are still adjusting, searching for the Final Answer to replace our lost gods, as Jaynes, in the last sentence of his book, admits he has been doing throughout.

Jaynes's metaphorical realm is social interaction. The public interactions of humankind provide both the motivation to consciousness and the terms in which consciousness emerges. Consequently, the causes of change are external, adaptive, and social. We needed to be able to deceive once trade reached a certain level, and then we needed to be able to deal with deception. We had to cope with the social pressures produced by roaming bands of displaced strangers. While Jaynes does not deny the importance of innate capacity, he imagines language too as developing in response to social needs.

Jaynes's theory is much closer to the theories of traditional social science than any of the others I have discussed. It would make sense to try to compare Jaynes with Vico, or with Toynbee, or to see if Talcott Parsons's model of social determinants is consistent with Jaynes's ideas on the common origins of society and consciousness. All these theorists share a model based on the dynamics of social interaction. Because they share assumptions about the causes and processes of change, they talk about the world in the same terms and may be usefully compared.

Freud was not (or professed not to be) greatly bothered that the anthropology on which he based his theory of the primal horde had passed out of fashion. He was not talking in the same terms as the anthropologists anyway. Psychic development, not social history, supplied the facts he was at pains to understand. In fact, in several works he interprets social history in terms of the findings of psychoanalysis. From Freud's point of view, psychoanalysis validates social history, not the reverse.

Freud's arguments are certainly open to criticism—but not from the points of view assumed by any of the other theorists I have described, if the criticism is to make any sense. The question of who among Jung, Freud, or Jaynes has the right approach to the evolution of the psyche reduces to a comparative evaluation of alternative realities. They speak from different worlds and cannot understand one another. Certainly Jung and Neumann understood one another well, and I imagine that their conversation with Teilhard, had he been allowed to publish in time to set the talk going, would have been friendly, or at least marked by mutual comprehension. I would like to call romantic the way Jung, Neumann, and Teilhard describe psychic evolution. They write in the romantic mode. Freud writes in the high mimetic mode, Jaynes in the low mimetic.

The distinctions among the metaphorical realms of the evolutionary theorists are more confusing than those among their causal processes. Yet it is just here that most attempts to describe world views have begun. To do so is a mistake. Both Freud and Teilhard use the language of biology. Yet in these cases as in all the others, their language is profoundly colored by causal process assumptions. Freud speaks in terms of physical structure, especially of the primitive stages of structural development. Freud's intention is to explain the present through the persistence of the past. When Teilhard speaks of developing physical structure he means to indicate the direction that future developments are likely to follow. In a teleological system the same terms can be used to different ends than when they are used in a system governed by primal causation. Similarly, when Jaynes speaks of mythology it is as evidence of the state of psychic development of the mythologizer, and as a record of the nature of social interaction. For Jung, on the other hand, myth means more than we can understand; it refers not to a social reality but to a condition of our being with which we are called to come to terms.

When two people think they are speaking of the same things and are not, the discussion is likely to be heated. Attention to the causal process assumptions underlying the speech may avoid blows. Frye's modes, which act as alternative experiential realities, seem fundamentally to be expectations that experience is arranged in one way or another. The modes are characteristic of all narrative, whether scientific or fictive. Motif analysis, which rests on metaphorical organization, is incapable of distinguishing true universes of discourse. No motif index can capture fundamental narrative patterns. Vladimir Propp's *Morphology of the Folktale* does not distinguish clearly between motif and process stage. Therefore, his analysis of narrative patterns loses itself in alternative motif strings for the same process.

I would like to return to the temporal orientations of the modes. If Jung, Neumann, and Teilhard are future oriented, Freud's conception of development is rooted in the extra-individual past, and Jaynes's in the pressures of the present. For Freud, the present is experienced and has its effect in terms prepared by the distant past. The individual is prisoner of something he is beyond any of the choices he has made. Jaynes conceives of the mind as changing in response to conditions in the present. For Jung and his modal associates, we are changed by a pressure to become whole—a pressure that comes both from within and from without, including extra-human reality.

Definitions of what we fundamentally *are* follow. In the romantic mode, we are individuals confronting our own complex being as we move toward psychic wholeness. Parts of our psyches, such as the strange figures who populate our dreams saying and doing things we did not expect and could not predict, may form within our larger selves to oppose our development or to help us along. There is a skull around romance. In the romantic mode our confrontations are finally with ourselves.

In Freud's high mimetic mode, we exist as members of a family unit, conceived in terms not of public presence but of ancient and impersonal identity. That family bears within it the freight of oedipal contradictions that the human mind has accumulated over thousands of years of experience. If in romance we confront ourselves, in high mimesis we confront the father, the mother, the sister, the brother, and we confront them in the nakedness of our primal drives.

In the low mimetic mode we are what our society makes of us. Low mimetic theory generally has little interest in the unconscious. When it is discussed, it is taken to be more a nuisance than a source of ultimate truth or of dark fate. For Jaynes, a low mimetic theorist, dreams, paranoia, and poetry are atavisms to a time before consciousness, when our right hemispheres spoke to us in conditions of stress. In low mimesis we confront

Reproduced in E. H. Gombrich (5) from *Die Fliegenden Blätter*

FIGURE 3. Rabbit or Duck?

other people; our identity is public. Families are described in terms of normal desires and fears in the present.

Because of the contrasting causal modalities, meaning arises variously in the modes. In low mimesis, meaning arises from human intention. In romance, meaning arises from human choice in the context of a universal and unified teleological movement toward wholeness. In a high mimetic world, meaning is immanent in the deterministic operation of unvarying principles of order.

The three categories of analysis can provide alternative explanations for the same experience—say, a dream—but none will provide a means of judging the ultimate validity of its analysis. We can choose to pitch our tents in one mode or another, but our choice cannot, by any criterion I can imagine, be defended by value terms having their reference beyond the chosen modal universe, because validity will necessarily be defined with respect to modal norms. We can choose to understand experience in terms of a drive to become something, but the romantic choice does not invalidate Freud; further, it cannot supply the terms of a meaningful critique. From the point of view of romance, Freudian theory pays attention to the wrong kinds of things with the wrong kinds of arguments; from the point of view of high mimesis, Jung does the same. The two are in different universes. I believe that the analogy to figure 3 is simple but relevant.

We can make of figure 3 a rabbit, a duck, or, if we are particularly skillful, nothing but an abstract pattern, but we cannot have it a rabbit and a duck simultaneously. Further, we cannot decide to keep it a rabbit and forget the duck once we have noticed both possibilities. The other possible reality obtrudes itself whether we will or no.

Similarly, once we have read Jung well, we can no longer live in an exclusively Freudian universe (and vice versa). Surely much of the bitterness of the continuing Freud-Jung polemic derives its heat from the obtrusive pressure of the competing mode of experience.

Frye has two modes other than the ones I have mentioned so far: irony and myth. Our ability to perceive figure 3 as a meaningless linear configuration has its origin in Frye's ironic mode. In terms of causal process, irony assumes contingency, an ultimately directionless universe. In irony we stand alone, as in romance, but without a meaningful inner movement. We end by confronting the baselessness of being. Irony is somewhat dislocated in time. Future and past do not really matter since nothing essential ever changes. For that reason the present, too, is indifferent.

Frye's fifth and last mode, myth, is not an analytical mode but a mode of perception this side of or beyond analysis. Myth is the mode of ultimate meaning, not of analysis. Nebuchadnezzar's dream, a sentimental myth (a myth perhaps sentimentalized in the text we have), presents its own analysis. One could perform analytical operations on the myth (its textual history, its relation to other myths of historical order, its internal dynamics), but when we read it as myth it presents itself as the ultimate referent of meaning.

Irony, too, is anti-analytical, but for opposite reasons. Derrida's "Speech and Phenomena: Introduction to the Problem of Signs in Husserl's Phenomenology," for example, yields a vision of fragmented verbal existence, not an analytical system. Irony is much better at critique than at constructive analysis. We will never be treated to a systematic exposition of the evolution of consciousness in the ironic mode. In a thoroughly contingent universe all systems are human projections, games we may choose to play or not as we wish with no consequence either way save the possibility of self-deception.

If myth and irony are out of the analytical picture, and if other modes are not lurking about unnoticed, every attempt to analyze the evolution of the psyche—or to analyze historical process in any manner whatsoever—will be romantic, high mimetic, or low mimetic. I propose that the modes define an exhaustive classification. When all possible relationships and connections are meaningful, we are in myth. When none are, we are in irony. In between we may be oriented to the future (romance), to the past (high mimetic), or to the present (low mimetic). We may let out part of the territory for subdivision, but insofar as causal process may be characterized by temporal orientation the modes define a continuum along which all causal processes must lie.

Frye's progression of historical modes fetches up in irony, at which point a literary culture disintegrates. Irony would then seem to be a sign of a cultural apocalypse. But an ironized existence has often been seen as one ripe for the emergence of another mode. As Frye observes of modern literature, "Irony descends from the low mimetic: it begins in realism and dispassionate observation. But as it does so, it moves steadily towards myth, and dim outlines of sacrificial rituals and dying gods begin to re-appear in it. Our five modes evidently go around in a circle" (1969, 42).

The Book of Job moves from the mythic prologue in heaven, through Job's ironic ruin in which his life becomes an unearned series of disasters, to his confrontation with God. In the enormity of his unjust suffering, Job breaks through the floor of irony into myth.

Similarly, Apuleius's main character in *The Golden Ass* breaks through the depths of his misery, trapped in an ass's form and degraded beyond endurance despite the animal freedoms at first offered by his transformation, into the presence of Isis.

St. John of the Cross recorded that in the dark night of our soul we are most likely to come across the blinding white light of the Divine Presence; Spenser's Red Cross Knight's hand must be stayed from suicide by Una in the Cave of Despair before he can conquer the dragon, just as every traditional Christian must come to a firm conviction of his or her state of sin before salvation is possible.

Enlightenment comes to the Zennist only when body and mind are cast off. Jung, the *Tao Te Ching*, and Ursula K. Le Guin all affirm that the left hand of darkness is light. Irony is not necessarily the sink of human thought but may afford an occasion for paradoxical returns.

In Thomas Pynchon's *Gravity's Rainbow* as in R. M. Rilke's *Duino Elegies*, an enormous and terrible angel, a possibility of order beyond human thought or hope, broods over the dark world. In these texts of transformation I see hope that our culture need not disintegrate into the ironic vision, as Nebuchadnezzar's dream might suggest. Seeing the world well in terms of one of the modes delivers great intellectual satisfaction and constitutes an endless project of cultural exploration; to glimpse the possibility of one world, one mode, transformed into another takes the intellect to the point of paradox.

Are we bound to the modes in our experiences of the world, then? I believe that we necessarily are. We cannot experience the world as an instantaneous rabbitduck. However, we can realize how we have seen things and thus achieve an allowance for difference.

The theorists I have described here tell stories intended to be true. In their narratives, no less than in our dreams, we imagine and incorporate new ways of being. In the resolutions of their stories are enacted our transformations in time.

The dream of Nebuchadnezzar is written from the point of view of myth in which all experience coincides. Short of that unreflective vision, the figure's metallic and earthen form might serve as a metaphor not only of the discontinuities of successive experience but of our diverse ways of being in history.

All the theorists of consciousness imply stories, and that implies the plot snake, as in Jung's plot of analysis. Freud's story of the psyche: first there was a primal horde. The sons murdered the father, but then they turned on one another. They had to select one among them who then himself became vulnerable. At last the incest taboo broke the cycle.

Jaynes's story: first we responded to voices that directed us as if in a dream. Then we had to direct ourselves in order to hide our intentions, and the voices were invested in a few powerful leaders. But the voices broke into a confused and ominous babble and finally ceased, except in extraordinary circumstances. We became dependent on ourselves.

Jung's and Neumann's story: first we existed in an unconscious unity with the world. Then came a breakthrough into cognition of self and other, which meant a traumatic separation from the parent, leading to a feeling of great power that we finally have to recognize as belonging to an extrapersonal level of identity.

Teilhard's story: first there was blind matter, struggling toward consciousness, which was achieved at a historical crux when tangential (thermodynamic) energy was transformed into radial (psychic) energy. But the newly conscious humans understood themselves to be autonomous and isolated from the ground of their being. After great suffering, and always with the possibility of failure, they anticipate the emergence of their unity (now consciously experienced) in the Omega Point.

These stories are implicit in the theories. Their narratizations of our location in time follow the plot snake and reflect our life cycle on a large scale indeed. To describe in detail the narratives in the various modes is the task at hand. Finally, the plot snake is too crude a tool to deal with actual narratives, for every narrative imagines a universe, and that means at least one causal modality. Plot process is specific to mode except for myth and irony. Ironization and mythicizing are operations that get performed on the processes of the remaining three modes, just as deconstruction ironizes prior texts or as Nebuchadnezzar's dream mythicizes a low mimetic cultural progression.

Table 1 summarizes the complete system of modal plot processes. At the high generalization level of narrative mode, it is intended to account for the plot structure of every narrative that has been or will be produced.

TABLE 1   Summary of Modal Plot Processes

General Process Stages

1.	2.	3.	4.	5.	6.
Initiation. Energy is loosed	Burnt fingers. Energy felt in random, confused way	Temporary binding. Energy subjected to unstable binding	Infernal vision. Energy demonstrates its potential for disruption	Final binding. Energy bound	Termination. A stable world beyond the work may be suggested

Modal Process Stages

Mode						
Romance	The call	The ordeal	In retreat	From the depths	Identity	Return
High Mimesis:	The violated ceremony	The fragmenting family	The climax	The straitened course	The way it is	The reflective survivors
Low Mimesis:	The other side of the fence	Social blunders	Simple solutions	Isolation	The firm society	Picking up the fallen standard
Irony	The opening door	The falling rain	A break in the clouds	Return to 2		

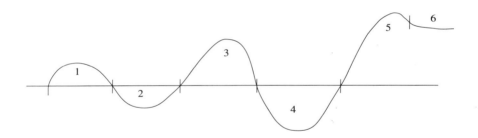

3

Low Mimesis

I SHALL ANALYZE one installment of the old "All in the Family" series and *She Stoops to Conquer* as two models of low mimetic plot process. I chose "All in the Family" because I hoped the reader would be familiar with Archie and Edith, and because it has dated in interesting ways. Recall of the specific episode is not necessary. In fact, since I only need a shared context and a sample plot, it would make little difference if I committed errors in transcribing the installment I am using.

"All in the Family": Low Mimetic Plot

The initial episode of "All in the Family" for the 1977–78 season ran an hour on the evening of 5 October. The numbers attached to the paragraphs in the following summary refer to the plot snake stages.

1. Archie Bunker visits Kelsey, recovering in the hospital from a heart attack. Kelsey has put his bar up for sale. He tells Archie (who works on a loading ramp) that he, Kelsey, was a working stiff too before he borrowed money to buy the bar. Archie is fascinated.

2. Edith Bunker does not share Archie's enthusiasm for the bar and, in a pillow-talk scene, alienates him by telling him that he is too old to start over. Archie blunders through an interview with a black female loan officer at the bank. (His crudity is almost savage.) He has to get Edith's signature on a mortgage note for $20,000 on their house so that he can buy the bar. Edith, horrified at the threat to their financial security, refuses.

3. Archie forges Edith's signature, quits his job, and buys the bar. He conceals all this from his family.

4. But the assembled family (especially Mike, the Bunkers' son-in-law) drags the truth from Archie. Edith is aghast and wounded.

Archie and Edith's relationship is deeply threatened, perhaps ruptured permanently. Archie leaves home.

5. Mike convinces Edith that Archie's dream of independence
   deserves support, even at the risk of their financial security. Edith
   walks into the bar while Archie is supposed to be going over inven-
   tory but is actually grieving over his breach with Edith. They make
   up.

6. Edith decides that since she is a partner in the bar, she will redec-
   orate—nice curtains, pictures of little animals. Goodhearted, naive
   Edith does not realize that the Mob requires Archie to use their
   cigarette machines. Archie is exasperated.

Archie's purchase of Kelsey's bar is a particular kind of temporary
binding. It solves the problem that has driven the plot to this point—
Archie's desire to change his life. But it provides only a temporary and
unstable solution, for to solve matters in this way Archie endangers his
marriage, which perhaps means more to him than the fulfillment of his
original desire. The only time we see him in his new bar without Edith, he
is not enjoying himself. So if his purchase of the bar is a binding of his original desire, it is a temporary and unstable one. The succeeding part of the
story must provide the final binding, during which the fulfillment of his
desire is consistent with the other impinging conditions of his existence.

The first paragraph provides the initiation: some novel condition is
introduced into the universe of the story. Archie, seeing what is on the
other side of the fence, is fascinated by the prospect of changing his life by
buying the bar. The plot enacts the process by which his desire is accommodated in the world of "All in the Family." In that sense Archie's desire
might be said to drive the plot.

In the second paragraph Archie's desire begins to bump things around.
The unfortunate loan officer has no previous or future connection with
the series, but she gets in the way of Archie's desire and social blunders
ensue. Edith is aghast at the implications of Archie's new obsession. In
this burnt fingers stage of plot, Archie's desire is making itself felt in a
fairly random and confused way.

Past the temporary binding (the third stage, when he buys the bar),
Archie's desire shows just how much disruption it can wreak on his life in
the fourth, infernal vision, stage of plot. His desire does its worst: it
destroys his identity as head of the family. It has led him to betray his wife.
Edith is right to kick him out. Although the average viewer knows that

with a full year of episodes to go Edith and Archie must get back together, at this stage it seems as if they have become permanently alienated, for Archie has violated their relationship on a deep level. The two are isolated, bereft of their normal social context.

Only Mike's sanity and Edith's magnanimity are capable of healing the breach in the final binding, thereby reestablishing a firm society. Mike reminds Edith of her crazy uncle who bought a car dealership and made a fool of himself in midlife. Does Archie not deserve the right to make a fool of himself, too? Edith has the strength of character to allow Archie this flaw among his many others.

Everyone who watches an episode or two of the series realizes that Edith is kinder, wiser, stronger, and generally a better person than Archie (who nonetheless holds the affection of the implied viewer). But a given of the show is that Archie will seem to have the upper hand. The last paragraph of my outline reestablishes the conditions under which the series is to continue, the stable social scale of "All in the Family." For in the final binding Edith has attained an uncomfortable superiority. She is the one who has made room for Archie's criminal foolishness, who is large enough to come to Archie and forgive him. How can this person be called "dingbat" (Archie's usual insult)? Only by grace of the termination stage of the plot, in which a stable world is reestablished by Edith's display of frivolous naïveté and by Archie's exasperated reaction, which gives the sympathetic viewer a comfortable feeling of amusement. We know where we are again. The fallen standard of society has been grasped again and advances.

When I saw and transcribed the "All in the Family" episode under discussion, I was thirty-five. Now at nearly fifty I find myself emerging from an unaccustomed attraction to sports cars and prepared to feel a different kind of interest in Archie's midlife crisis. I understood when first I saw the show what Archie was going through and felt that he was basically right to make the move (even if culpable in his method), but my sympathy was with Edith. I now feel closer to Archie. The plot has shifted slightly for me. A Chinese viewer (I speak from my own limited understanding of Chinese culture) would be more likely than I (either at thirty-five or at fifty) to see Archie as selfish and deeply at fault in his betrayal of family values. A person who had never seen any television situation comedy before and who had no sense of the continuity of the sitcom or of the established relationships in "All in the Family" would have a diminished expectation that Mike would be able to patch things up between Archie and Edith (indeed, would not know who Mike was) and would not comprehend that a reassuringly normal situation was being reestablished in the termination phase of the plot.

Finally, in the years since the episode was produced, our culture has changed sufficiently so that (to the best of my memory) the debasing of Edith in the termination is more objectionable now than it was then. While we always knew she was not really a dingbat, it did not formerly make me as uncomfortable to hear her called so. (I would enjoy arguing whether this represents a change in my maturity or in our culture, and, in principle, the argument could yield a conclusion; please accept the change as cultural.) As the way we consider the acts of the characters changes, so must the plot. In ways external to the text, the plot has changed in the years since it first appeared. The hypothetical naif and Chinese readers always would have experienced a different plot.

The sitcom's plot has six process stages, so far defined as those shared by all narratives that achieve a firm conclusion. But on that level of generality little can be said. I would like to discuss the features specific to the episode as a low mimetic narrative.

Archie's desire drives the plot. Not all plots are driven by desire. *Star Wars* is driven by the Force, *Waiting for Godot* by anxiety. Proximate causation rules in the plot line given for the episode. No drive from the primal past, no mysteriously meaningful chain of circumstance moves the plot forward. The values of the plot are social. People exist in their identity as members of society. While the setting is a family, the relationships are those that are familial but public.

The mode of every "All in the Family" episode I recall is low mimetic; each takes place in the universe as named in that mode. Low mimetic plots are driven by simple emotions capable of social expression: desire, fear, grief, greed, curiosity, nostalgia. If the terms are understood capaciously, the driving energies of low mimesis may be said to be desire and fear. A particular process, a specification of the general process stages, is fit to bind such energies. A model of low mimetic plot follows.

(1) *The other side of the fence.* Some desire or fear arises in characters that will be bound by the process of the plot. (The grass on the other side of the fence should not be imagined as always greener; sometimes it bears grazing monsters, and the fence is rickety.)

(2) *Social blunders.* Intrusion of the desire or fear into the world of the work arouses confusion; normal social bonds are threatened. In situation comedies this is typically the time for one-line zingers. The plot often

seems to be taking off in directions that are not pursued. Characters often seem to blunder about. (I mean my process stage labels such as "social blunders" to be mnemonic aids; the process stage is defined by energic change, not by the presence or absence of literal blundering, which is a motif capable of appearing at any point of any kind of narrative.)

(3) *Simple solutions*. Some sort of temporary but unstable arrangement subjects the fear or desire to a temporary binding. The contradictions that cause the solution to be unstable are at the heart of the problem posed by the intrusive energy. The simple solution threatens social bonds. The main problem with Archie buying the bar is that he has other obligations, other people who are involved in his decisions. To take the leap he imagines endangers his family along with him.

(4) *Isolation*. Once the implications of change are fully developed, the desire or fear shows the full range of social damage it is capable of working in the plot; the energy that drives the plot is fully manifest at this stage. We see the implications of Archie's desire—it could mean destroying his place in the family. He would be isolated from them.

(5) *The firm society*. Fully manifest, the desire or fear can be bound. The result is not necessarily happy. In the remake of *Invasion of the Body Snatchers*, the body snatchers win. But in our sitcom episode, values expand to encompass Archie and his fulfilled desire in the family unit.

(6) *Picking up the fallen standard*. Society marches on (even if it has become a society of body snatchers). Some sort of stable world is re-established.

A sitcom is under special pressure to return to the givens of the show. "All in the Family" was mildly atypical in the way it allowed change from episode to episode (Mike and Gloria get married, have a child, get divorced; Archie and Edith develop an on-screen history that informs later episodes). Top sitcoms such as "WKRP," "M*A*S*H," and "The Mary Tyler Moore Show" usually allowed only minor personnel changes from show to show. Archie kept his bar through Edith's death and the next incarnation of the show, "Archie's Place."

"Cheers" and "All In The Family" with their continually developing story lines are thus more like the comic strips "Gasoline Alley" and "For Better or Worse" than like "Peanuts" or "B.C.," which undergo little change. Sometimes the process of change becomes orderly in the manner of a plot snake, as in the episodes around Mike and Gloria's divorce, but more usually the change is too gradual to develop a dynamic of interest and so does not become plotlike. Of course, such TV serials as "thirty-something" or strips such as "Prince Valiant" are organized around larger units than the episode and present a sequence of full plot shapes.

A Modal Analysis of *She Stoops to Conquer*

Oliver Goldsmith's *She Stoops to Conquer* also exhibits the low mimetic plot form. It is an ancestor—a blood relative—of modern situation comedy. As with other members of its great family of commoners, the play has seemed to no one to need a great deal of explaining or to hold many mysteries. Comment has been limited primarily to its sources in English and French drama, and to its status as autobiographical fantasy (for example, see Sells 1974, chapters 14 and 26). As simple as the play is, however, it presents complexities of plot not found in the "All in the Family" episode.

The reader of the play has a sense of *a* plot, of a single, unified action. The play does not break into pieces. Yet several stories seem in progress. Kate Hardcastle woos Marlow successfully. Tony Lumpkin wrestles free of his mother's plans for him and comes into his inheritance. Constance and Hastings get married and retrieve her jewels from Mrs. Hardcastle. Mr. Hardcastle acts mostly in the stories of others, but Mrs. Hardcastle has her own schemes and desires, thwarted in the end. This play cannot be said to be driven by the overt desires of a single character as can the "All in the Family" episode.

Plot process can be distributed within a work; plot can be shared among characters. One character might desire something that is achieved by another character. A motion may be completed by a character who knows nothing of the beginning.

I hope the reader will mentally star the preceding paragraph. It took me long to realize the full independence of plot process from character. So long as plot is assumed to be a character's story, confusions will multiply. Whatever comments I make in this book implying that plot is character-specific arise from the necessity of expressing dynamics in terms of the foci of our attention, the characters. The truth is otherwise. Of course, plot process often *does* follow the action of a character, making us less wary for the next fluidity of plot dynamics.

Even the prologue can, in our experience, condition the central events of the text. The actor/producer David Garrick's prologue provides a frame situation in terms of which we approach the play. If we know enough to understand the prologue, enough of the context of the play, we know what the play represents for Goldsmith—a triumph over Garrick's failure to produce the play and over the reluctance of Colman, who did produce it, as well as a chance for desperately needed money and for respect.

Goldsmith had announced in a magazine article that comedy had strayed from its proper course in England. His play was to correct the mistake. Goldsmith's treatment of the Voltairean distinction between laughing and sentimental comedy (*She Stoops to Conquer* was to restore the laughing type to its proper ascendency) has the air of a public relations ploy, even though the issue itself is significant in cultural history. Like a good ploy Goldsmith's article invites us to play a game in which we sample the product and make the invited decision.

The prologue assumes that we recognize the connection between Goldsmith's aesthetic campaign and his personal situation—his tender literary honor and even more tender financial standing. It asks us to judge: is Goldsmith, the failed doctor of dubious medical credentials, a literary quack as well?

> Excuse me, Sirs, I pray—I can't yet speak—
> I'm crying now—and have been all the week! . . .
> The Comic muse, long sick, is now a dying! . . .
> One hope remains—hearing the maid was ill,
> A *doctor* comes this night to shew his skill.
> To cheer her heart, and give your muscles motion,
> He in *five draughts* prepar'd, presents a potion:
> A kind of magic charm—for be assur'd,
> If you will *swallow* it, the maid is cur'd:
> But desp'rate the Doctor, and her case is,
> If you reject the dose, and make wry faces!
> This truth he boasts, will boast it while he lives,
> No *pois'nous drugs* are mixed in what he gives;
> Should he succeed, you'll give him his degree;
> If not, within he will receive no fee!
> The college *you*, must his pretensions back,
> Pronounce him *regular*, or dub him *quack*.

To enjoy the play is to be generous and indulgent to its author. Our kindness may awaken; at the other extreme, some may feel that contempt for Goldsmith that he aroused and can yet arouse. His medical practice failed after a druggist refused to fill one of Goldsmith's prescriptions in which, apparently, "pois'nous drugs" *were* mixed. Whether we are sympathetic to Goldsmith, hold him in contempt, or find ourselves indifferent to him, our reaction will color our experience of the play.

Jonathan Culler maintains that to explain a plot is to explicate our sense of what the plot was (1975a, 127). Since we intuitively know that such things as prologues and descriptions of scenery are not part of the plot, Culler believes, we explain nothing by discussing these features when we are trying to understand the plot. His analogy is to linguistics. We experience a literary work by virtue of our competence; the task of the literary theoretician, like that of the linguist, is to map the competence—to make explicit what we already knew.

I agree. But the string of bare incidents we tend to produce when asked to describe a plot displays about the same level of sophistication as grammatical explanations by people who (unlike Culler) have only a superficial knowledge of linguistics. Although I do not ordinarily describe the prologue when asked to recount the plot of *She Stoops to Conquer*, it is yet a necessary adjunct to my experience of the plot.

And yet it is not part of the plot per se, for it is not itself directly part of a process of change. Let us call such textual features, when considered for their implications concerning our experience of the plot, *textual conditions* of the plot.

Prologues, epilogues, and, within the text, the induction commonly provide such conditions. Yet what looks at first sight to be idle chit-chat, the mere providing of an introduction to a character, may introduce a tension that initiates the action. Certainly such is the case when Gloucester introduces his bastard son, Edmund, to Kent in *Lear* 1.1. The casual conversation of Mr. and Mrs. Hardcastle on which the curtain rises in *She Stoops to Conquer* provides another example of the inclusion within the plot proper of what would ordinarily be called *induction*.

As the plot proper opens Mrs. Hardcastle expresses to her husband her restlessness and dissatisfaction with life in the country, and they argue a bit over Tony Lumpkin's rude and unruly ways. Mrs. Hardcastle's yearning for a different life is never fulfilled, at least not by her. She thinks she would be satisfied by a London life, but her provincial dowdiness is engrained. Her desire becomes legitimate in the two girls, Kate Hardcastle and Constance Neville, who are right to pursue London gentlemen as mates. They will escape the provincial life, to a degree; Kate will carry a bit of it with her, also engrained.

Provincial values are affirmed in Kate, Mr. Hardcastle, and Tony. Kate dresses provincially (to please her father) and in the London fashion (to please herself) by turns. She wins Marlow by modulating from provincial simplicity to urban sophistication by degrees. Mr. Hardcastle, an exemplar of one set of positive provincial values, understands his wife; he sees through her and is not corrupted by her foolishness, can rise above her machinations. He is, as he says, fond of her. When she has been misled by her son and lies abject in the mud begging for mercy, he raises her without sentimental commiseration but with proper compassion.

Tony is the energetic center of the play. He wishes for the tavern life and for freedom from his mother. Through Mr. Hardcastle's eyes we at first entertain the possibility that Tony is a selfish lush, a lout who is both ignorant and content to remain so. But he has resources. He is the leader of the tavern party at the Three Pigeons; he controls the action from his first entry whenever he is on stage. The only time he is beleaguered is at the pit of the plot's infernal vision, when Marlow has mistakenly returned the jewels to Mrs. Hardcastle and Tony's illiteracy has exposed Hastings's letter to his mother's eyes. But Tony provides the means by which the plot is resolved. Unwittingly, with his practical joke, he has also provided Marlow with the means to approach Kate.

Tony is the extreme of one sort of provincial ideal of ignorant but canny good spirits. He stands on the opposite side of Mr. Hardcastle from Kate. Tony is strenuous, celebrative. Without some of his energy, Mr. Hardcastle's contentment would become complacency, his discernment turn more completely toward sentimental nostalgia. Not that Mr. Hardcastle changes or requires redemption by Tony (though he does come to take Tony's part against Mrs. Hardcastle). In the pattern of oppositions and modulations by which this plot progresses, Tony and Mr. Hardcastle are brought into harmony. Mr. Hardcastle would act to moderate his daughter's sophistication and his stepson's wildness but is neither very serious nor effective in either direction; in a sense, he is moderated by them both.

Mrs. Hardcastle's restlessness is a kind of vulnerability, then, a foolishness and a source of affectation in her that is bound in the course of the plot both by Kate's and Connie's successes in fulfilling their legitimate urban aspirations and by Tony's success in establishing himself in the sort of rural life he desires. Mrs. Hardcastle herself remains unsatisfied and unredeemed, a wielder of parental authority, a character type to be neutralized in Roman comedy as in the modern sitcom. Mrs. Hardcastle has concealed from Tony his majority and withheld Connie's patrimony (both her jewels and the approval that her dead father had bestowed on Hastings). She tries to force Connie and Tony to marry in spite of their wishes and their consanguinity, at least partly because she covets Connie's jewels.

Much of the play turns on mistakes and transformations of identity, as its subtitle (and Goldsmith's working title) implies: "The Mistakes of a Night." Kate's country resourcefulness and lack of pretension allow her to approach Marlow, but what he takes as her identity is known by the audience to be partly a perception of her genuine earthiness, partly a deception engendered by class stereotypes. Neither her town clothing by day nor her country clothing at night encompasses her. Marlow, as well, has two poles of identity, but is engaged in an uncomfortable class-based straddle. In his tavern identity he can be sexual but respects neither his partners nor himself. In his formal identity he is rigidly moral, inarticulate, and antisexual (women are forbidding to him—it seems that Kate squints). Kate does not disappear into her roles as he does. She is able to preserve her integrity and can switch back and forth to please her father and her own aspirations.

Kate would be pleased with an appropriate husband but maintains a careful reserve with her father so as not to commit herself too far ahead of time. She discerns in Marlow more good than the audience may perceive; in a way, she creates Marlow's generosity by creating the situation in which it emerges. Up to that emergence, in the final binding of the plot, Marlow has been cold, lecherous, haughty, insensitive, and foolish ("At the Ladies Club in town I'm called their agreeable Rattle.") by turns. He arouses sympathy mostly in his friendship for Hastings and in his role as discomfited victim.

Connie is unsure whether to abandon her true love or her fortune. She returns in the final binding to secure both. Subterfuge is the worst of her situation—she is forced to pretend affection for Tony and to conceal her relationship with Hastings. Escape from subterfuge is her deliverance, as it is Kate's.

The first stage of the plot, *the other side of the fence*, includes Mrs. Hardcastle's exchange with her husband and son, Mr. Hardcastle's announcement of Marlow to Kate, and Connie's discovery that Hastings is on his way with Marlow. To be bound by the plot are the clash between rural and sophisticated values, and the desire of the women; the satisfaction of the desire is to provide the mediation of the opposition of values.

Tony begins the *social blunders* stage of the plot with a rural idyll in the

Three Pigeons, interrupted by the arrival of the haughty but dislocated and therefore vulnerable young gentlemen.

If Marlow and Hastings's sophistication is embattled, so is Tony's idyll. Tony's carousing, after all, is with unworthy and ridiculous fellows. The song he has composed rejects learning and religion. Neither, indeed, is affirmed elsewhere in the play, but the civilized values they represent will find positive embodiment in the young lovers. Somewhat like Tony, Mr. Hardcastle at this social blunders stage of the plot makes himself ridiculous with the servants by trying to ape London household manners.

Thanks to Tony's practical joke of leading the two young men to mistake Mr. Hardcastle's house for an inn, Mr. Hardcastle, Marlow, and Hastings mistake one another woefully. In the beginning Marlow has at least the solidarity of common misunderstanding with Hastings, but after Hastings learns the truth from Connie, Marlow is isolated in his mistake. The embarrassment we feel for him is matched by the embarrassment he feels before Kate in their stiff interview.

With Hastings's enlistment of Tony in winning Constance, and with Kate's discovery that there is more to Marlow than she at first thought, the plot has passed the maximum of the disorder achieved (mostly by Tony) in the second stage and is moving toward the temporary binding.

In the third stage of the plot, *simple solutions*, Tony secures Connie's jewels and Kate establishes a flirtation with Marlow. Mrs. Hardcastle, the schemer against youth, is now isolated—Tony torments her, refusing to understand her as serious but constantly recalling her duplicity (which, after all, he has suggested).

The resolution achieved in the third stage is unstable in several ways. Connie has not truly gained what is rightfully hers but is simply receiving stolen goods: both the jewels and, as she intends, Hastings. Tony's ascendancy over his mother is temporary and is based on deception, as is Kate's relationship with Marlow. The young people have forced solutions that constitute them as a social group based on fraud. They have, however, achieved the literal associations they wish, both with one another and with the jewels. The balance of the play will be filled with the comic pain generated as they accommodate themselves to the larger adult world.

Isolation, the fourth or infernal vision stage, threatens to dissolve all that has been accomplished in the third stage by applying larger social standards to the simple solutions. Marlow cannot entertain the possibility of marrying a barmaid. Mr. Hardcastle attempts to eject Marlow from the house. Mrs. Hardcastle discovers Hastings's true intentions with regard to

Connie and his true opinion of Mrs. Hardcastle when Tony's illiteracy (a weaker side of rural values) allows the letter to fall into her hands. In the depth of the dissolution of the associations of the young people, all are estranged from one another or, in the case of Connie and Hastings, prepared for separation.

The last speech of act 4, the one of Tony's that begins "Ecod, I have hit it," marks the turn from the maximum disorder of the fourth stage and begins the movement toward the final binding stage, *the firm society*. Hereafter affairs cease disintegrating for the young people and move toward success.

Yet confusion, crossed purposes, mistaken outrage, and fear still dominate the play in this period of transition. Sir Charles Marlow's arrival has been the occasion for an offstage enlightenment of Marlow as to his real location, but he still has not connected Kate with the poor relative he loves. The resulting confusion continues to disrupt the reconciliation toward which Mr. Hardcastle keeps trying to move. Mrs. Hardcastle is in for her worst hour, mistaking her husband for a murderous brigand. Wet and bedraggled, at his feet, risking her life to beg for that of the son who has so bamboozled her, Mrs. Hardcastle is experiencing the full effect of the unbound desire of the young lovers and of her son's wish for freedom from her. In this last swing of the fourth stage, desire as a centrifugal force expends itself, becoming tame and centripetal.

Kate stands somewhat apart from all this. Since late in the second stage of the plot she has been the only character who has always known as much as the audience, the only one for whom we possess no discrepant awareness. She alone can show to Marlow, and to the father, what he really is, eliciting his natural social identity.

The worst of it for Marlow is that he comes to feel that he must abandon a woman for whom he feels increasing love; the final binding is that he discovers in her his appropriate mate and in doing so finds himself freed into open discourse. Kate is addressed as she deserves. When Marlow first discovers whom he has been addressing, however, he is mortified: "I must be gone." His turn to acceptance of his new role is internal and silent; it happens while we are watching other characters.

Hastings's and Connie's return is the point at which the actual final bindings begin, the assertions of common sense, honesty, and social normality that mark the firm society stage. Tony discovers that he has come into his majority and releases Constance from his mother's plan to marry the two of them; she is therefore free to marry Hastings. Marlow accepts his new social identity and proposes to Kate, whose father joins their hands. *All disguises are penetrated, all hypocrisies revealed, as is typical in this stage of a low mimetic plot.* Society reconstitutes itself about the marriages. Only Mrs. Hardcastle remains frustrated in her antisocial greed.

In the final speech of the play, Mr. Hardcastle welcomes the lovers to society at large, thereby providing a slight termination stage, *picking up the fallen standard.* Perhaps no more elaborate termination is necessary because we have never moved far from the norms of society. (Such was not the case in the "All in the Family" episode.)

Goldsmith's epilogue, like the alternative epilogue written by J. Craddock, returns the audience to the theater, delivering us from the stage space and time, and projects the characters of the play on that world. While Craddock has Tony gloating about spending his inheritance with Bet Bouncer in London, Goldsmith brings on Kate to deliver the ages of the barmaid, a parody of Jaques' "ages of man" speech in *As You Like It.* In the last two lines, "The Bar-maid now for your protection prays, / Turns Female Barrister, and pleads for Bayes," the reference to Bayes identifies Goldsmith with Dryden in a self-deprecating key, *Bayes* being a satirical name for Dryden and a patronizing term for a playwright generally. The epilogue asks us to judge the play—and it puts Goldsmith in the company of Shakespeare and of Dryden, if diffidently.

The interactions of the characters in *She Stoops to Conquer* are not as subtle as they are in, say, *Hamlet* or *War and Peace.* Motives and strategies are clear. Yet psychological theory can help us to a new sense of order even here. Eric Berne's analysis of social transactions provides a useful way to describe Kate's management of Marlow. Transactional analysis, as described in chapter 2 of *Games People Play* (1964), identifies three positions from which we speak to another person: our parent, our child, or our adult. In their first formal interview, Kate and Marlow speak parent to parent. Apparently it is the only way Marlow knows to speak with a woman of his class.

Courtship and sexual play are difficult when one severely moralistic parent speaks to another. The role is so uncomfortable for Marlow that Kate has to keep up both ends of the conversation. Deliverance comes when Kate, mistaken for a barmaid, stumbles across Marlow's greedy and sensual child. Addressed by his child as if she were one, she responds appropriately, establishing a level of communication with Marlow on which courtship is possible. Her project for the rest of the play is to gradually change her level of discourse, and thereby Marlow's response, until she speaks and is answered as an adult, with the proper ulterior transaction between children in the background. That is, by the end she and Marlow have reached the capacity to make objective appraisals of reality (their adults speak to one another) and still to convey the messages of playful attraction to one another (the ulterior child-child transaction).

Throughout the play, characters act from ulterior motives. Hastings flatters Mrs. Hardcastle. Tony and Connie pretend to flirt with one another, and Tony torments his mother. The process of the plot undoes such pretense. In Berne's terms, all characters are game-free by the end.

Neither Freud nor Jung can provide an elucidating terminology so apt to the play as that of Berne, for he like Goldsmith is speaking of a world in which our primary identity is social, and in which meaning arises from human intention. Third Force psychology—that of Maslow, Horney, and Erikson, as described and applied by Bernard Paris in *A Psychological Approach to Fiction* (1974)—is no doubt a low mimetic tradition within psychology more complex than Berne's theory and more appropriate to complex low mimetic narratives such as those of Austen, Dickens, and Tolstoy.

Throughout the universe of low mimesis identity is conceived in terms of public presentation. In this mode, as in Third Force psychology, we are whatever we are in relation to other people. Whatever other possibilities a work might suggest belong to another mode, perhaps to another plot line. To the extent that we take seriously the dimension of *Great Expectations* in which Pip, having formed his identity on a mistake, has no identity at all but remains under the gravestone's shadow in which Magwitch finds him, to that extent we are experiencing the ironized plot line of the novel. To the extent that Marlow is unredeemed by Kate and has been alienated from friend and family by the absurd behavior to which his mistakes have led him, the play is ironized. Different productions and different readings of the play will emphasize the ironic plot line to different degrees, no doubt in accordance with the identity themes Norman Holland describes in *The I* (1985).

I do not find a significant romantic plot line in *She Stoops to Conquer*. To the extent that we experience the play as organized by meaningful coincidence, we experience the play as a romance. From the standpoint of the low mimetic plot line, romantic causal processes of meaningful coincidence seem weaknesses in plotting, and if they are prominent the play may seem to depend too strongly on mere coincidence. The word *improbable* in a critical commentary on a low mimetic narrative is generally a signal of this sort of modal clash. As for *She Stoops to Conquer*, "One forgets that the plot is littered with absurd coincidences and improbabilities because the farcical scenes and vigorous characterizations are so full of juicy vitality" (Halsband, 1966). So the play is not entirely free of romantic causation. Still, neither the romantic nor the ironic dimensions of the play are pronounced; the low mimetic plot line is so strong and so central in the play that other plot lines only hint at undeveloped possibilities.

The suggestion of open-ended savagery in Tony's treatment of his mother is an undeveloped high mimetic direction of the plot. The same sort of excess is a vicious dimension of Marlow's and Hastings's ungentlemanly treatment of Mr. Hardcastle, a suggestion of one generation trampling on another also found in Mrs. Hardcastle's treatment of the children. Behind such destructive energy lie the primal constants of our identities within families that often dominate high mimetic works. Such irrationalities seldom trouble modern sitcom families. Archie Bunker's conflicts with his family are explicable in terms of present situations. The high mimetic conflicts of *She Stoops to Conquer* help to give it complexity and depth. Perhaps without its high mimetic features the play would not have been so persistent a part of the English curriculum and would not be—as it is—so frequently revived.

I have been treating *She Stoops to Conquer* in detail. Perhaps brief and broad comparisons can be useful as well.

Some Modern Low Mimetic Political Novels

Goldsmith's play and "All in the Family" belong to one family of low mimetic narratives, the Terentian comedic tradition. (I confess I have no generic map of the territory, just some standard genealogies. I only assume that a generic map is possible; I do later provide such a map for the romantic mode.)

I have worked out a plot description that is general to six novels: John Steinbeck's *Grapes of Wrath*, Ignazio Silone's *Bread and Wine*, André Malraux's *Man's Fate*, B. F. Skinner's *Walden Two*, George Orwell's *1984*, and Upton Sinclair's *The Jungle*. With limited groups of works, it is often possible to discern plot organizations within the divisions of the six-part process structure. I have numbered these more articulated stages and superimposed the six-part structure, which still serves to describe the broad entropic organization of the works—they still follow the plot snake.

Too, one can specify the form that a process stage takes, as in the following first plot stage description. The purpose of the analysis that follows is to reach a formulation of the plot process common to a group of works so as to highlight family features. One holds the narratives up to a window to see where the light comes through.

The other side of the fence. (1) The ambiguous gathering: The gathering is often a party that does not go right, or a meeting of old acquaintances in sad or uneasy circumstances. The openings serve to suggest lost or unachieved social tranquility.

Social blunders. (2) The good old days: A sexual or familial idyll, or a flashback to a period when the group was happily established. (3) The big picture: The work broadens to detail the disintegrative pressures in the society at large that were responsible for the uneasiness of the initial scene. The "blunders" of this stage belong to present society, destructive to the idyll. Agents of the society at large threaten the integrity and freedom of central individuals; impersonal and collective interests force life awry.

Simple solutions. (4) Voyage: Important characters undertake physical journeys, hoping to establish a better society but encountering some of the destructive elements. This stage in all the novels serves to establish a broad social perspective. The problems addressed by the books are not those of personality, nor are they local.

Isolation. (5) Disintegration: The group fragments or the members lose contact with one another. (6) Isolation: The hero, isolated from all normal sources of social support, gathers himself to reconstruct society. (7) False societies: Groups based on predatory or otherwise unsatisfactory premises form and dissolve. The individual in this process stage struggles heroically but finds that no one person can achieve a solution, or even escape.

The firm society. (8) Illumination: The hero achieves a vision of a possible new order, or a social contact leading to the establishment of a valid group. The novels assert collective values, for good or ill.

Picking up the fallen standard. (9) The new social order moves ahead, for better or for worse.

Obviously, the "valid group" and the "new social order" are malevolent in the dystopias. Most of the novels manage to be affirming even in the face of the triumph of capitalism, fascism, or the darker side of human nature. *Grapes of Wrath*, *Bread and Wine*, and *The Jungle* associate their central characters with the figure of Christ. Suffering thereby becomes an affirmation of positive values and a promise of redemption. In *1984* and

Man's Fate suffering demonstrates only the futility of action in a society gone bad at the core. Malraux's novel is strongly ironized.

The family of works suggested here is large. It includes Pietro di Donato's *Christ in Concrete*, John Dos Passos's *U.S.A.*, almost anything by Ayn Rand, most of Aldous Huxley, and a vast number of muckraking, socialist, fascist, and otherwise activist works going back to Thomas More's *Utopia* and beyond. However, *Utopia* will not fit the nine-part process described above; neither will Dr. Samuel Johnson's *Rasselas*, William Thackeray's *Vanity Fair*, Pynchon's *The Crying of Lot 49*, or, to my knowledge, any other narrative of broad social analysis written before about 1860 or after about 1960. The six novels (and their generic peers) might be located within the larger group of utopian and dystopian narratives as the novels of modernist commitment. Were I to continue this study in their direction, I would look at the literary reflexes to the rise and decline of fascism.

The purpose of generalizing about groups of works in this way is to suggest an approach for genre studies. I imagine a similar analysis of an appropriate group of picaresque works that would act as an adjunct to Claudio Guillen's (1971) list of picaresque characteristics. One purpose of such a study would be to trace historical change.

I have tried to describe in this chapter a highly generalized plot process and to make it possible for others to discern this process in low mimetic works. I should say that analysis of a plot process is hardly ever simple. The compensation is that by the time you know the process, you have come to understand much about the work.

I recommend beginning by identifying the temporary binding. Where, in the work at hand, do things seem to have been resolved, only to fall apart most disastrously? (The temporary binding itself provides the disaster—Archie forges Edith's signature; the lovers of *She Stoops to Conquer* engage in deceit.) If you can say what seems to have been bound there, why it falls apart, and how it is finally resolved and can further identify the significant textual and extratextual conditions of your experience, you understand the plot.

4

High Mimesis:
Freud, Sophocles, Shakespeare,
and the Plot of Analysis

HIGH MIMETIC NARRATIVES are organized by original causation: some changeless principles of order emerge and assert their power in the present. The only high mimetic works I know tell of an emerging and destructive family dynamic.

Among literary works, high mimetic plots are most readily found in the tragedies of Golden Age Greece and Elizabethan England. I do not understand why literary works with primary plots in high mimesis are not to be found in other times. Frye argued in the first essay of *Anatomy of Criticism* that modes characterize cultural stages and that high mimesis is most characteristic of the ages of Sophocles and of Shakespeare.

Secondary high mimetic plot lines abound in literature of all forms and types, however, and this century has seen the birth of a major extraliterary genre of high mimetic narrative: Freudian analysis. In psychoanalysis, the patient and analyst collaborate in producing a retrospective story of the patient's life. The notion that psychoanalysis is a kind of narration has intrigued many people inside and outside the psychoanalytic community. Donald Spence, a psychoanalyst, provides a good bibliography of the psychoanalytic literature on the topic in his *Narrative Truth and Historical Truth* (1982).

Spence is concerned that the status of psychoanalysis as narrative brings its validity into question. Any narrative told of external events involves the following factors: (1) the event; (2) the perception of the event; (3) the memory of the event; (4) internal verbalization of the memory (encoding); (5) transmission of the coded memory; and (6) reception of the story (decoding). At every step lies an opportunity for distortion. We cannot know the event directly and simply but only through the mediation of our sensory abilities, which represent the event through patterns (perhaps neural patterns in our brains) not found in the event itself. Our memories are endlessly creative. In psychoanalysis, encoding is conditioned by expectations and assumptions that, as Spence says, are never made entirely explicit. In any case, all encoding consists of symbol and meaning systems with their own distorting constraints. Narratization, as I am attempting to specify here and as Spence is aware, carries its own set of templates, projections, and filters.

I have no insights that will aid in settling—on Spence's terms—the questions he raises about the truth status of the psychoanalytic narrative, but I do intend to address the nature of that narrative and thereby to obviate his objections. Spence's book provides an example of the difficulty attendant on raising questions of truth in cross-modal analyses.

Peter Brooks's *Reading for the Plot* (1984) analyzes Freud as narrator and applies Freudian dynamics to the representation of plot in general. I have adopted his general approach with modification.

The analyst Roy Schafer in chapter 3 of *A New Language for Psychoanalysis* (1976) discusses psychoanalysis in terms of Frye's historical modes. In specifying the modal structure of psychoanalysis, I am following a direction he indicated. I am interested in the nature of the psychoanalytic story, in the shape of its plot, and in its relationship to narrative fictions.

One central psychoanalytic narrative is Freud's most complete case history, that of the Wolf-Man. It was written in 1914–15 and translated into English as *From the History of an Infantile Neurosis* (Freud, vol. 17). Freud's purpose in this work is to describe the childhood neurosis of which the presenting symptoms of the adult Wolf-Man were developments. However, Freud does give enough of the analysis itself to allow a reconstruction of its broad outlines.

Freud's account is supplemented by a volume titled *The Wolf-Man by the Wolf-Man, with The Case of the Wolf-Man, by Sigmund Freud and a Supplement by Ruth Mack Brunswick, Foreword by Anna Freud, Edited, with Notes, an Introduction, and Chapters by Muriel Gardiner* (Gardiner 1971). In this book the Wolf-Man himself provides accounts of his life and of his experiences with Freud. Ruth Mack Brunswick reports on her analysis of the patient twelve years after he had completed analysis with Freud, and Muriel Gardiner writes of her long association with the Wolf-Man, extending to 1971, the time of the book's publication.

The Wolf-Man, son of Russian aristocrats, entered analysis with Freud in 1910 at the age of twenty-three following years of unsuccessful and often bizarre therapies. He remained in analysis with Freud until 1914. His principal presenting complaint was that "for him the world was hidden in a veil, or that he was cut off from the world by a veil. This veil was torn only at one moment—when, after an enema, the contents of the bowel left the intestinal canal; and he then felt well and normal again" (Freud, 17:75). He was able to achieve a bowel movement only with the help of an enema. He was often depressed and felt unable to respond emotionally to others. The condition had persisted for some years. Toward the end of the analysis, the Wolf-Man's bowels resumed their normal function as Freud had dramatically predicted, and the other symptoms abated, at least for several years.

The analysis uncovered an anal erotism generated by a homosexual fixation on the father, complicated by castration anxiety. Freud's understanding of the case has been challenged in the last decades. Louis Breger's *Freud's Unfinished Journey* (1981) is a general critique of Freud's case histories and another consideration of psychoanalysis as narrative (using Thomas Kuhn's term *paradigm* to describe the nature of the psychoanalytic story, a term used in the same way by Spence). Breger refers to a 1979 thesis written for the Southern California Psychoanalytic Institute by E. C. Peck in which Peck, as Breger reports, deemphasizes the primal scene and calls attention to the succession of governesses who cared for the Wolf-Man, some of whom were quite sadistic. The Wolf-Man himself, in conversations toward the end of his life with an Austrian journalist, had harsh words for all his analysts (see Obholzer 1982). Certainly the most compressed and dramatic critique of Freud's Wolf-Man narrative comes from the preface to Jeffrey Masson's *Assault on Truth* (1984). He reports seeing unpublished notes by Ruth Mack Brunswick to the effect that, unknown to Freud, the Wolf-Man was anally seduced as a child by a close relative (1984, ix). The effect is to call into question the form of Freud's case narrative, although not his understanding of the general nature of the neurosis. I will return to Masson's news. However, I am concerned here primarily with the analysis as developed by Freud and his patient—with the story as they generated it.

The Wolf-Man gets his name from a dream he had, close to Christmas, at the age of four. The window of his bedroom slid open to reveal five or six white wolves staring at him fixedly from their perch in a walnut tree outside. He awoke in terror. Interpretation revealed that the dream represented the primal scene, parental intercourse *a tergo* (on hands and knees), which the Wolf-Man witnessed at the age of one and a half and interrupted by passing a stool. The dream provided the means in the analysis for the Wolf-Man to confront his infantile relationship to his father.

In the final stages of the analysis, the Wolf-Man recalled (or recalled and constructed) a childhood scene with his nursemaid Grusha. When he was two and a half years old, he had urinated on the floor upon seeing Grusha *on her hands and knees* cleaning with a scrub brush. She had responded, "no doubt jokingly, with a threat of castration" (Freud, 17:50–51).

Freud does not clarify to what extent the micturition and resulting threat are constructions and to what extent they are actual memories of the patient. Spence in *Narrative Truth* (1982, 117–22) analyzes the confusion as an instance of the potential mischief played by the narrative impulse. Since I view the narrative impulse as shaping the entire psychoanalytic situation, I am not alarmed by the confusion and view it only as the result of Freud's indifference to the distinction between memory and construction, both of which have approximately the same truth value for him in the therapeutic situation and play the same part in therapy. The key point is that the construction must be validated by the patient as accurate. If the patient does not recognize the experiential accuracy of the construction, it is abandoned. Peter Brooks discusses a related point, approving of Freud's honesty in leaving the undecidable question "fantasy or memory?" open and explicit (1984, 277).

The Grusha memory or construction provided the final link between his fixation on his father arising from the primal scene of parental intercourse *a tergo* and his later compulsive choices of sexual partners. (He fell promptly in love when he saw a woman, particularly a serving woman with an ample posterior, on her hands and knees.) The scene with Grusha also accounted for several neurotic symptoms seemingly unrelated to this infantile attempt at seduction.

The analysis ended soon after the Grusha materials emerged. "When once the Grusha scene had been assimilated—the first experience that he could really remember, and one which he had remembered without any conjectures or intervention on my part—the problem of the treatment had every appearance of having been solved. From that time forward there were no more resistances; all that remained to be done was to collect and to co-ordinate" (Freud, 17:94–95).

One interesting feature of Freud's account of this case is the extent to which it is clear that the creation of the psychoanalytic plot was a collaboration between Freud and the Wolf-Man. Freud commonly provided constructions to be verified or rejected by the patient. Freud says the primal scene (of parental intercourse), so prominent in the case of the Wolf-Man and in others of Freud's cases, is *always* a construction, never a memory of the patient (17:50–51). Yet the infantile memory of parental intercourse is commonly demanded by the materials of the analysis—the dreams, memories, symptoms, and associations out of which the analysis is built. The primal scene is a common motif in the Freudian plot.

Freud is apprehensive, even anguished, that enemies will seize on the constructive nature of the primal scene to deny the validity of psychoanalysis absolutely. The Freudian plot is a way of perceiving oneself in a certain relationship to the world, in a certain mode that is to say, and the primal scene is an expression of a relationship to one's parents that is common in Freud's kind of life plot. In the psychoanalytic plot, the primal scene has a truth value analogous to that of a memory. Memories themselves, as Freud demonstrated again and again, are always to a greater or lesser degree constructions in service of our need for continuity.

If Masson's information is accurate and the Wolf-Man was anally seduced as a child, the Grusha memory might remain important but might play a different role. I imagine a narrative in which the Grusha memory is a screen serving to negate the memory of seduction. The seducer is not an adult but a child in the screen memory; the Wolf-Man in his memory of urinating before Grusha is not the seduced but the seducer. He remembers the seduced not as a child but as an adult, not as a male but as a female. The role of the memory as important to the Wolf-Man's object choice remains. Castration anxiety attaches not to the constructed threat but to the role forced on the Wolf-Man by his seduction. The primal scene is less likely to be significant in the narrative that forms around the new information. Assuming that both Masson and Brunswick are accurate in reporting the new piece of information, the narrative generated by its inclusion in the case might be said to be more adequate to the best that we know than the one reported by Freud. However, the mode and general form of the narrative remain the same in the two narratives.

The causal process fundamental to high mimetic narrative is primal causation. Changeless principles beyond the reach of present human decision govern all action. High mimetic narratives usually record an individual's discovery of his or her inclusion within these principles—of the way in which his or her existence has been ordered beyond choice or knowledge. The discovery may destroy or strengthen its discoverer. The roles of hero and victim in high mimesis are as close as Oedipus and Macbeth, both men who believed that they could control the condition of their existence. Indeed, every high mimetic hero/heroine is both hero/heroine and victim to a palpable degree.

Shakespeare's high mimetic plays are *Hamlet, King Lear*, and *Macbeth*. They, along with *Oedipus the King*, are driven by libido—by energy of a generalized sexual character that has no natural object. In all the plays, the energy expresses itself in intergenerational predation or in incestuous desire and repulsion. The high mimetic process in these plays, as in psychoanalysis, is that of an emerging and destructive family (or inter-generational) dynamic. In table 2, I list the basic plot processes, along with summaries of the main plot lines of several plays and of the Wolf-Man case history.

The general high mimetic plot process, second down in table 2, describes the way libido is bound in narrative fiction. The high mimetic process is a specification of the general process: the violated ceremony is the way initiation works in high mimesis, the fragmenting family is the burnt fingers function in the high mimetic mode, and so forth.

In *the violated ceremony*, the first function of a high mimetic plot line, social order and continuity (often some sort of actual ceremony asserting these features) are disrupted by an unexplained intrusion. Among the high mimetic fictions used as examples in table 2, three are disrupted by super-natural intrusions; the fourth, *King Lear*, is disrupted by a directly mani-fest breakdown in the orderly succession of generations. The disruption begins to alienate family members from one another in the second stage, *the fragmenting family*. In the third, *the climax*, intergenerational hostility takes on definite form. Beyond this point, the traditional climax, the action seems inevitable as intergenerational lust and predations emerge in stage four, *the straitened course*, to destroy the family unit. Stage five, *the way it is*, often involves suicide, murder, and mutilation. The underlying structure of the narrative has emerged in contradiction to familial peace and the human moral order. In the last stage, *the reflective survivors* survey a desolated world in which they must live with a more or less chastened view of the human condition (even, I would argue, in *Macbeth*, the most anomalous play of the group).

I hope that the examples in table 2 will make the scheme I have just described intelligible to those who recall the plays. The analyses given are in the most general possible terms; I provide them only to illustrate the central tendencies of high mimesis. The plot model allows far more detailed treatment.

I propose that psychoanalysis develops a narrative of the patient's life,

TABLE 2. Parallel Processes in Psychoanalysis, *Oedipus the King,* and Other High Mimetic Plays

Process Stages	1. Initiation	2. Burnt fingers	3. Temporary binding
High mimesis	The violated ceremony	The fragmenting family	The climax
Freudian Psychoanalysis	Neurotic disruption	Anamnesis; initial resistances encountered	Transference develops; patient begins to provide interpretations
Wolf-Man case history	Presenting symptoms: depression, physical complaints. "A veil over reality"	Anamnesis: Wolf-Man emotionally detached from analysis	Initial resolution of wolf dream; provided partially by the Wolf-Man
Oedipus the King	Theban plague; Oedipus investigates	Tiresias talks; Oedipus quarrels with Creon	Oedipus hears how Laius died
Hamlet	Hamlet Sr. appears on the battlements	Hamlet talks to ghost, torments family members	Hamlet kills Polonius, pleads with mother
King Lear	Lear divides kingdom	Goneril & Regan reject Lear	Lear goes mad on the heath
Macbeth	Macbeth is tempted by witches	Macbeth quarrels and plots	Macbeth murders Duncan

Process stages	4. Infernal vision	5. Final binding	6. Termination
High mimesis	The straitened course	The way it is	The reflective survivors
Freudian Psychoanalysis	Patient confronts early death/sexual materials at root of neurosis	Transference resolved	Patient discharged
Wolf-Man case history	Grusha material produced spontaneously; Wolf-Man faces attraction to his father	Transference (incompletely) resolved	Wolf-Man discharged (later analyses)
Oedipus the King	Oedipus discovers the truth	Jocasta's suicide; Oedipus blinds self	Oedipus accepts banishment
Hamlet	Hamlet evades Claudius, struggles in grave with Laertes	Gertrude, Laertes, Claudius, and Hamlet die	Fortinbras takes command
King Lear	Cordelia is captured with Lear	Evil siblings, Cordelia, and Lear die	"We who are young..."
Macbeth	Equivocating visions; a father, mother, & son are killed	Lady Macbeth's suicide; Macbeth is defeated and killed	Macbeth's head is displayed

perceived as true, within which the present and the past come to make sense. In the writings of Freud and in his direct tradition, that narrative is in the high mimetic mode, driven by libido and embodying an emerging family or intergenerational dynamic essentially similar to that of high mimetic fiction.

Jacques Lacan espouses a point of view based in irony, a psychology best equipped to deal with plot lines driven by anxiety. Karen Horney's psychology is essentially low mimetic: it imagines us primarily in our social identity, as beings motivated for the most part by simple desire or simple fear. Because their psychologies are based in modes other than high mimesis, I do not consider these psychologists, or others for whom our fundamental life plot is other than high mimetic, in the *direct* Freudian tradition.

In the last chapter of *A General Introduction to Psychoanalysis*, Freud says that analysis "falls into two phases. In the first, all the libido is forced from the symptoms into the transference and concentrated there; in the second, the struggle is waged around this new object and the libido is liberated from it" (16:455). I intend the general structure of psychoanalysis described in the third item in table 2 to be consistent with this statement, with Freud's case histories, and with full-term psychoanalysis in general (that is, in the direct Freudian tradition).

The disruption occurs outside the psychoanalytic setting, for which it provides the occasion. From the point of contact between analyst and patient at the beginning of the second stage, the plot process is shared—a collaboration. The interaction of analyst and patient is itself an inextricable part of the plot. The transference, a necessary feature of full-term analysis in which the patient projects important persons from the past onto the analyst, is both a feature of a relationship in the present and the means by which the past emerges—a function of the plot process.

The patient is increasingly active in the psychoanalytic plot, increasingly the discoverer of the story. Certainly as the analysis proceeds the patient learns how such a story might be constructed, but to overemphasize the developing narrative skills of the patient is to ignore the importance of the coherent story that has emerged with the transference and that drives the process on to its own discovery. Like the Wolf-Man, Oedipus, Macbeth, and Hamlet are each in their own way—Hamlet more passively, Macbeth more grimly, and Oedipus more excitedly—fascinated, almost possessed, by the unfolding logic of events. The Wolf-Man, who in the beginning of the analysis had been remarkably passive and disengaged, increasingly became the discoverer of his own story as the analysis progressed.

My process scheme obviously comes from my work on fictional plot. It could hardly have arisen from the psychoanalytic materials I have examined. Complete case histories of psychoanalyses are not published. (Vamik Volkan's 1984 case history *What Do You Get When You Cross a Dandelion With a Rose?* is a happy exception; Paul Dewald's 1972 *Psychoanalytic Process* is more complete but unwieldy.) Psychoanalysis is highly and obscurely personal. Analysts report that the true shape of an analysis is buried in a mass of materials that it took them years to sort out and that would make similar demands on the reader. (Anna Freud discusses this point in her introduction to Gardiner's *Wolf-Man*, explaining why that case history has been so central to the training of psychoanalysts: it is one of the most complete case histories available, as well as being instructive and well written.) I hope that my plot scheme is sufficiently true to the shape of an analysis that some development from it might alleviate at least the psychoanalyst's problem of representability.

Werner M. Mendel, in explaining the nature of that phenomenological development of psychoanalysis called analysis of existence, states that "personal lived history is constantly rewritten and is seen as active behavior in the present" (Natterson 1980, 392). Notice that Mendel says that we are always acting within some life story. I must now introduce a complication noticed by psychoanalysts Schafer and Mendel and the larger part of the literary community in this century: the fundamental ambiguity of texts. Stories are polysemous, including life stories.

A story, as E. M. Forster says in *Aspects of the Novel*, is a sequence of actions; a plot adds causality (1927, 26). But as David Hume noted in the eighteenth century, causality is at least partly in the mind. In our understanding of a text, as of an event, causal relationships, and therefore plot forms, may vary for a single text. From reader to reader, textual features may differ in prominence or in their understood relationship to extra-textual features. Any text—including a set of memories and conjectures—can be the occasion for multiple plots. I have spoken as if all possible experiences of the works I have named were exhausted by my process descriptions. But they are not. *King Lear*, it is often noticed, has many connections with the romances. One can experience it as a failed romance, or as a parody of a romance; it has a romantic plot line as well as the high mimetic plot line I have described. Perhaps I can claim, at most, that the dominant plot line of the play is high mimetic.

Psychoanalysis, by analytic techniques and by the expectations generated in the direct Freudian tradition, elicits from the materials of a life a
high mimetic plot line. The analysand's life would furnish others if considered in the context of another mode.

Psychoanalysis, then, makes *one type* of life story explicit. It is a story
the patient is driven to discover. Perhaps I see and read high mimetic
tragedies and take them seriously because they help me name my experience of the world in the high mimetic mode. *King Lear* is one of the ways
I am in the world. My aesthetic distance from the work is a measure of the
degree to which Lear's experience is not my own; my interest in the story,
the energy I bring to it, is a measure of the degree to which it is my own.

The juxtaposition of the high mimetic fictions with the Wolf-Man case
history suggests comparisons that help make sense of both classes of narrative. The plague at Thebes at the opening of *Oedipus the King* and the
appearance of Hamlet's father on the battlements are like the presenting
symptoms of a neurosis. They are experienced as disturbances imposed on
the characters that cannot be ignored, that demand that the characters
discover the stories behind them. These stories are already extant but
unexpressed, as tacit as is the story behind an unexamined neurotic
symptom. Normal life may no longer be pursued while the plague per-
sists, while the ghost walks.

Conversely, the presenting symptoms of a neurosis are like the beginnings of a plot: an announcement of an undiscovered order of meaning
that the patient must confront if normal life is to be resumed. In the
second stage of the high mimetic plot, knowledge emerges in fragments,
often to be rejected, ignored, or misunderstood. Characters and patients
are carried along somewhat unwillingly by the pressure of the plot.

In the temporary binding stage, the knowledge emerging in the plot
focuses the energies of the characters and of the patients. What is now a
quest acquires a focus—the dream of the wolves, Laius's murder. The
heroes act with a new purposiveness.

The climax passed, the patient and the analyst are locked in a truly joint
enterprise for the first time, just as the general family of a high mimetic
fiction becomes increasingly involved in the progressive destruction that
increasing knowledge brings. In analysis the family is in a sense present
for the first time, as with the development of the transference neurosis the
analyst becomes a screen on which the patient will project significant
others, usually family members.

It is in the final confrontation that psychoanalysis and high mimetic fictions differ most markedly. In both, the characters are delivered into the present, the past having become fully manifest. But the characters of high mimetic fiction emerge maimed if at all. In fiction, when (for example) one must confront the actual mother, or the real presence of the murdering uncle who is both one's double and one's antagonist, the final confrontation demands resolutions as serious and as drastic as the now manifest conflict. But in the analyst, the patient confronts only the projection of significant family figures engendered by the transference neurosis. As the need for such projection is resolved by the knowledge it brings, the actual analyst can emerge. The patient's motive for destruction becomes weaker as the transference resolves and the analyst becomes more the screen and less the projection.

Freudian high mimesis traces events of the present back to some original cause: a traumatic set of typical, historically determined events in early childhood that lies at the root of our personality and of our difficulties. Freud, in *The Psychopathology of Everyday Life*, maintains that it is impossible to think of a number wholly at random; there are no accidents in the psychic life, no absolutely innocent dreams, no indifferent choices. Certainly Oedipus and Macbeth are caught along with the Wolf-Man in this sort of deterministic trap. In *Hamlet* and *Lear* the tropism of high mimesis for original causation shows up in several ways, among them the heavy use of plot parallels. The similarities of identity and action among Hamlet, Laertes, and Fortinbras, as between Lear and Gloucester, enact the high mimetic mood of being caught in some disastrous script unfolding before the characters. The origin of the script is within the patient, the characters, and yet it is the result of no conscious choice.

Perhaps part of the underlying form of *Hamlet* is that the main character identifies with his uncle and wishes to approach his mother sexually. We have been made familiar with the textual clues supporting this argument in Ernest Jones's *Hamlet and Oedipus* (1976), and by that work's supporters and detractors. Hamlet, perhaps, cannot take vengeance because Claudius is his dark double. Only when dying will Hamlet take Claudius with him.

But the secret at Hamlet's heart, the tune to be played on the stops of the recorder, sounds only partially when *Hamlet* is juxtaposed with other high mimetic narratives and hardly at all from the play in isolation. Parallels and Oedipal analysis do not exhaust the latent content of the action. There are gods down there. The Oedipus story itself is primarily one of reconciliation to the divine presence in one's life, of acquiescence. High mimetic heroes enter into unity with what is, generally, beyond the grave. Hamlet's impatience with the dreary furor of the world carries him toward unity; the secret of life lies in death. Hamlet and his double, Laertes, struggle in the grave until they enter it at one another's hand.

The end of *Hamlet* is a lost inheritance reclaimed by one who has allowed himself to be directed in violence by his uncle, one who appropriates Hamlet to his own identity, that of a soldier. But Fortinbras is mistaken. The price of his manliness, his effective succession to a murdered father, is a narrowness of soul. Fortinbras, Polonius, and Rosencrantz and Guildenstern all bear inadequate visions and expectations that do not encompass the play's presentation of experience. They all assume that meaning is a matter of will—that life is a matter of intention, decision, and desire. They bring low mimetic expectations to high mimetic events and dwindle before the reality. Within the world of high mimesis, the low mimetic world seems bounded in a nutshell. (The converse is equally true.)

At the center of all high mimetic narratives lies a chill. In a mechanistic world, human aspirations and values are contrivances, artifices of no interest within the actual order of events. *King Lear* will not affirm that loyalty, love, sacrifice, morality, and wisdom do or do not exist. Evil does play itself out. No forces of predation are left at the end, no human reason for England not to be well run. But the setting within which humans play their part is indifferent. Does the storm on the heath express Lear's wrath, working it on the world, or is it his punishment? Neither. In the face of the heavens we are reduced to pitiful, unprotected things. To whatever dramas of mercy, villainy, justice, or kingship we wish, we must supply the roles. Human evil works toward its own destruction—but because of a contradiction in the human heart, not because of a divine moral order that ensures victory for the good. Edgar can praise the just gods only because he forgets that he set up the lesson in benevolence himself. What Lear comes to understand on the heath does not protect him from sorrow; misanthropic cynicism is no refuge for a great soul. Gloucester is preserved by an illusion of grace only to die on hearing the truth. Lear thinks he has seen through to what humans are but recognizes neither Edgar nor Kent.

Dr. Johnson's pain at Cordelia's death was at least partly moral. Edgar has stage-managed a low mimetic happy ending in which we must concur so far as we are incapable of absolute cynicism. To the extent that we acquiesce in the low mimetic assumptions of the efficacy of human will we feel the impact of Lear's entry with Cordelia dead in his arms. It seems to come after the end, a supersufficiency of disaster. Cordelia had no need to die.

Lear alone among these high mimetic narratives questions whether events have any order whatsoever beyond human contrivance. The question *is* open in the play. Too many dimensions of order press themselves on us for us to experience *Lear* as wholly ironic. Not least are the double and parallel actions. One father echoes another; the set of brothers mirrors the sisters. Gloucester and not Edmund has the stars right—if they portend the disasters he names in 1.2.101–14, they portend truly. Yet what principle of plot is satisfied by Cordelia's death? Absolute meaninglessness threatens to overwhelm the play. From such an ironic perspective, high mimetic mechanism collapses in on itself and causality loses direction.

Spence's critique of Freud in *Narrative Truth and Historical Truth* is based on assumptions general to ironic narration. A human being is essentially an isolated consciousness. The personality possesses no veridical core. Memory is a construction in the present. Experience has no essential meaning, no inherent order; all meaning is a construction in the present. For Spence, coincidence and chance underlie the sort of causal arguments made in psychoanalysis. Psychoanalysis under these ironic conditions would be a matter of the present, not of the past.

Freud's assumptions are quite different. In our identity we express a conscious-unconscious system, resting on racial memory, a common psychodynamics, significant past experiences, and a nexus of interpersonal relationships. Personality is epiphenomenal to early experiences and memories. Memory is an archeological enterprise. Meaning is discovered, not devised. Finally, Freud assumes as the primary causal modality pressures arising from early personal experiences in forms generated by hereditary psychodynamics.

Neither set of assumptions can be demonstrated to the exclusion of the other set. Yet both can be demonstrated in a limited way. Both constitute ways of looking at the world and are true to universes of experience, yet they are contradictory. Such is the nature of modal assumptions. Without them we have no bridge to experience. Yet they constitute exclusive universes. Narrative truth is a matter of modal coherence. Spence's objections to Freud reduce to a preference for ironic over high mimetic assumptions, just as Jungian critiques of Freud generally express a preference for romance over high mimesis and vice versa.

Most battles within literary criticism reproduce the same kind of clash. It is no good telling a poststructuralist that ironic mode assumptions about texts are misguided, and it is no good telling someone with differing modal assumptions that they are not. A proper criticism would make the assumptions clear—and stick to the texts for which those assumptions are most useful.

Bernard Paris in *A Psychological Approach to Fiction* (1974) argues for the specific applicability of Third Force psychology to low mimetic fiction. Freud's theories apply to high mimetic narrative. I would like to go further and say that Freud applies primarily in high mimesis. A Freudian perspective on main plot lines in other modes is bound to seem out of focus. Different frames for different modes. Hamlet and Orlando inhabit worlds organized disparately.

In his last theoretical work, "Analysis Terminable and Interminable," Freud remembered the effect of setting a time limit on the Wolf-Man's analysis. The ploy opened up what had become a blocked process and made a resolution possible. In modal terms, perhaps, Freud had forced a reinterpretation in high mimesis of materials that were threatening to yield an ironic plot line. (Roy Schafer [1976] has remarked the presence of both ironic and high mimetic elements in psychoanalysis; I am arguing that the elements represent diverging trends in treatment of the analytical material.) A high mimetic plot process reaches a firm conclusion. The modal shift to a closed form, high mimesis, saved the analysis from the ironic tendency to continual recurrence.

In the same article Freud pondered the tendency of the benefits of psychoanalysis to fade with time. The Wolf-Man himself required further treatment by Freud and by Ruth Mack Brunswick, who found him a borderline psychotic. Perhaps the plot of analysis becomes less adequate to the main character's need for coherence as the life situation changes. Perhaps other materials from the past, not considered or not emphasized in the previous life plot, demand attention. The patient may begin to perceive himself in a different mode. D. M. Thomas's 1981 novel *The White Hotel* is built on the discrepancy generated by setting a Freudian analysis in a romantic plot process. It might be useful for an analyst to decide at the beginning the modal needs of a patient, and to be aware of the inadequacy of any life plot to the total life situation.

Yet a story is no less necessary, no less saving, for its necessary limitation to a modal perspective. The Freudian analysis within *The White Hotel* is inadequate only from the point of view of romance, of the teleological dynamic the main plot line assumes, and not absolutely. Freud's analysis of the Wolf-Man met the needs of a life situation but not of all situations of that life.

In 1918 Freud wrote in "On the Teaching of Psycho-Analysis in

Universities" that "the psychoanalyst can dispense entirely with the University without any loss to himself" while, on the other hand, psychoanalysts have much to say to colleagues in other fields (17:171). Freud saw psychoanalysis as fundamental, primary, the source of illumination, a field that uses other areas of knowledge only as examples and matter for analysis.

Perhaps literary studies can repay some of the considerable favors done by psychoanalysis. A consciousness of the narrative qualities of an analysis, and of the narrative structure toward which psychoanalysis tends, can only increase an analyst's awareness of the analytical situation. Such knowledge must put the analyst more in control of the analytical relationship.

I wish to emphasize that from the point of view I am developing here Freudian analysis is neither more nor less primary than *Hamlet*. The Wolf-Man case history is not the key to *Hamlet*, nor is the reverse true, but, as culturally central high mimetic expressions of experience, each illuminates the other, and each has dimensions and concerns unshared with the other or, for that matter, with any other text.

Anxieties about the truthfulness of perceptions and memories are generally not helpful in high mimetic experience. Truth tends to become an internal matter, a conviction of fitness and of emerging pattern as much for Oedipus and Macbeth as for the Wolf-Man. In high mimesis as in romance, verification and conviction merge. In high mimesis, the order of experience arises from inside us out of an extrapersonal past. In romance, experience is ordered by patterns outside human intention, a dimension of order in which we are invited or impelled to create a future. In high mimesis we are constrained by the extrapersonal past. In romance we are drawn into the future.

5

Romance

By ROMANCE, I mean a narrative driven by a teleological dynamic in which meaning is constructed by the characters as they act in a framework of meaningful coincidence in accordance with or in opposition to an organized movement in the world at large directed toward some future state and determined by it. As loosely as the word *romance* has been used, it usually refers to the general body of works I wish to consider in this chapter. Harlequin Romances are, more properly, Harlequin Low Mimetics, but most of us would agree that *Star Wars*, *The Winter's Tale*, and *Sir Gawain and the Green Knight* are among the romances.

Romance in General: "Allerleirauh"

In "Allerleirauh" from *Grimm's Fairy Tales* the temporary binding comes when the little girl is discovered hiding in a hollow tree and given a place as a menial. She has escaped the attentions of her father and achieved a place in life, so that the initial problem of the plot is resolved, but she has the appearance of a contemptible animal and a degraded station, so that the resolution is only temporary.

The king who discovers her in the forest is easily mistaken on a casual reading for the king she has just escaped, her father. They are differentiated by no remarked characteristic—name, age, appearance, or behavior. Is the story then an incest fantasy?

Not in the main, the romantic plot line. Allerleirauh does not marry her father. She achieves an appropriate sexual identity through the transformation of those energies she has brought from her relationship with her father. A high mimetic plot would identify the two kings in a unity of incestuous desire that emerges to imprison the heroine.

Allerleirauh's father's attentions have both elevated her to supreme value (her cosmic dresses) and degraded her to bestiality (her coat of furs). To the world she is a hairy animal. Only her dresses, hidden away in a tiny nut, a kind of seed or potential, and the tokens she has brought from her father's house counter her appearance. In this romance, she is freed from the contradiction between undervaluation and overvaluation (internally, between aversion and desire), not destroyed by it. She is not caught within a preexisting order as in high mimesis but becomes a queen, the proper generational successor to her mother, through creative action in a context of meaningful coincidences that place her in the hands of a benign king who will elicit rather than demand her sexual response.

In a low mimetic story, she might have taken the golden ring, spinning wheel, and reel because they were especially valuable, or because she foresaw their utility. In that world, meaning arises from human intention. As it is she merely happens to take them, and they are just what she must have to symbolize her presence (beyond her degraded appearance) to the king. Meaning arises in romance not through intention nor through the operation of ineluctable law but through such fortunate action.

Like her, the three round objects are small, exceedingly valuable, and feminine. They bear a numen, at least for readers who remember Briar Rose's trance induced by an enchanted spindle, and the symbolism that connects spinning with feminine personifications of fate. The king slips her ring on the finger she has left in its underlying purity through his urgent importunity at the dance, which left her too little time for complete concealment. The chaste sexuality of the act, combining masculine and feminine in an image of innocent penetration in which her finger is the unwilling penetrator, both depends upon and is expressed in the marriage rite.

After the temporary binding in the forest, Allerleirauh, now on her own in the world, is responsible for her own salvation—partially. She is active in manipulating partial revelations of her presence (she attends the festivities in her splendid dresses and puts surprises in the king's soup dishes) but also energetic in concealing her true identity from the king. She needs to be discovered and cannot discover herself. Indeed, her actions seem unmotivated, as if she were acting from simple instinct. If her partial revelations of herself were merely cunning she would not so resist discovery. Further, the person who must discover her is easily confused with—a doppelganger of—the person who sent her into hiding in the first place, her father. He is an analogue of her father, and therefore an object of the original desire, but different, and therefore finally acceptable.

"Allerleirauh" is of type 510B in the Aarne-Thompson system and closely related to 510A, "Cinderella." In terms of plot dynamics at the generality level of the types, it is identical after the temporary binding. That means that the two tales are binding the same energy, obviously of an erotic nature. In "Cinderella," the heroine must deal with devaluation by the mother; in "Allerleirauh," with inappropriate sexual interest (over-valuation of a kind) by the father. The two tales as a diptych suggest a final unity between the two motivating teleological dynamics. They both end in the same place.

The active force that saves the heroine is much like the active force that threatened her in the beginning. The teleological force at large in the world that impels and pulls the heroine through the plot manifests itself as a drive toward nonbeing or its opposite, identity, according to the requirements of the plot. In *The Odyssey* Poseidon and Athene, the divine reason that Odysseus has so much trouble getting home (Poseidon) and the divine abettor of his return (Athene), are subsumed under a single cosmic order. Luke Skywalker of the *Star Wars* trilogy draws on the same Force (personified in its benevolent aspect by Obi-Wan Kenobi) that opposes him in the person of Darth Vader, his father, with whom he is reconciled in the last installment (to date). In the movie *The Dark Crystal* the kind, mystical ur-Ru and the evil Skeksis merge in the end to the same creature, an original unity reachieved in the plot. In Kurt Vonnegut's *Sirens of Titan* the teleological determinant of human history is called "the universal will to become" and, bottled, can be used to drive space ships. It shapes events with no concern for human welfare, and in that heavily ironized romance no Athene or Obi-Wan will lead the characters to an instauration or a new order. The greatest scope of benevolence in *Sirens of Titan* is to maintain or create healing illusions.

The teleological force that drives romance, then, generally appears malevolent to the main characters in the early stages of the plot. In some dark romances it is indifferent or malevolent throughout. When it threatens the security of the characters on whom the romance focuses or retards their progress, when it appears to wish to drag them back into oblivion or permanent childhood, it often assumes an identity separate from its more benevolent personifications. A common move for a romantic plot is to assert the final unity of the benevolent and malevolent sides of the teleological force. As in J. R. R. Tolkien's *Lord of the Rings*, the most potent creative power and its antithesis derive from the same source. Frodo and Gollum embody this ambivalence: Gollum is a hobbit degenerated in the service of the Ring of Power. When Frodo and Gollum destroy the Ring in Mount Doom, they annihilate the benevolent Galadriel's power as well as the malevolent Sauron's.

Sometimes the force driving romance assumes a unity internal to the hero. Sir Gawain finds that the threat he was confronting is finally from himself, as does Ged of Ursula K. Le Guin's *Wizard of Earthsea* and Gautama Buddha in his enlightenment. Odin and Christ hang on their trees as sacrifices to themselves. However, in "Allerleirauh" the driving force remains partially objectified in the persons of the kings.

The passive-aggressive behavior of Allerleirauh as she moves simultaneously toward and away from the king may look like the result of sexist traditions of female behavior. She seems unable to assert herself. Comparison with other romances indicates that the situation is more complicated (although, to be sure, sexual role conditions the plot, and sexual roles are culturally conditioned). The Grimms' tale "Iron Hans" makes an excellent double for "Allerleirauh"; in it a boy goes through sexual maturation. The peculiar behavior of Allerleirauh in the fourth, from the depths, phase of the plot is mirrored by the hero of "Iron Hans" as well as by every hero and heroine of romance. I would like to produce a kind of catalogue of plots, selected for cultural, temporal, generic, and presentational variety. The point is to illuminate such modal features as the passivity of main characters in the romantic infernal vision.

A Clutch of Romances

The same snake I used for low mimetic plot applies equally well as a basic figural metaphor for high mimetic and romantic plots (see fig. 4).

Process stage by process stage, I move through a large group of romances to indicate both the unity and the variety of romance. I am not attempting plot summaries. My notes are meant only to indicate the regions of change of direction in the plot lines. Also, while all the works listed have main plot lines in the romantic mode, most have secondary plot lines in other modes that I do not indicate here.

I hope to include a sufficient number of texts so that among them the reader will find several that are familiar. The works, in alphabetical order, and the abbreviations by which I shall refer to them, are: "Allerleirauh"; *Beowulf;* Arthur C. Clarke, *Childhood's End; Gilgamesh* (in N. K. Sandars's Penguin Books version); "Iron Hans"; Geoffrey Chaucer, "The Knight's Tale"; Tolkien, *The Lord of the Rings (LOTR)*; Jung, *Memories, Dreams,*

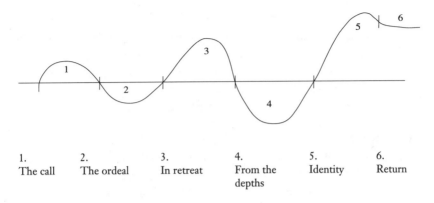

1.	2.	3.	4.	5.	6.
The call	The ordeal	In retreat	From the depths	Identity	Return

FIGURE 4. Romantic Plot Form

Reflections (MDR); Homer, *The Odyssey*; Herman Hesse, *Siddhartha*; *Sir Gawain and the Green Knight (Gawain)*; George Lucas, *Star Wars*; Shakespeare, *The Winter's Tale (WT)*; and Le Guin, *A Wizard of Earthsea (Wizard)*.

Stage 1. *The call.*

"Allerleirauh": Allerleirauh's father, reacting to the strictures of her dying mother, chooses Allerleirauh to be his new wife. *Beowulf:* (1) Grendel attacks; (2) Grendel's mother attacks; (3) the dragon is roused. (*Beowulf*'s plot is a threefold incremental repetition.) *Childhood's End:* The alien Overlords arrive to dominate the earth. *Gilgamesh:* Gilgamesh troubles his people with his martial and sexual energy; Enkidu is created as a solution. "Iron Hans": Iron Hans, who causes the king's men to disappear in the woods, is discovered beneath the waters of a lake and is captured. "Knight's Tale": Palamon and Arcite, imprisoned, spy Emily. *LOTR:* Bilbo relinquishes the ring and the mission of its destruction is pressed upon Frodo. *MDR:* Visions and secrets of Jung's childhood intimate a hidden world of meaning. *Odyssey:* Athene secures permission to help Odysseus; Telemachus leaves home, threatened by the suitors, in search of news of his father. *Siddhartha:* Siddhartha abandons his father and his position in life. *Gawain:* Gawain accepts the Green Knight's challenge. *Star Wars:* Luke stumbles on Princess Leia's plea for help. *WT:* Leontes' jealousy leads him to plot his friend's death. *Wizard:* Ged shows strange abilities with magic spells.

The beginnings are all unsought; indeed, they are forced on the main characters who are all to some degree objects of rather than creators of change. Leontes' jealousy, Siddhartha's dissatisfaction, and the desire of Palamon and Arcite arise within the characters as do the motive forces of low mimetic plots, but in the romantic plot line the characters are tools of their emotions, which are thrust upon them as if from outside. When Palamon spies Emily he cries out as if stung. Shakespeare, as is often remarked, softens the motivation given for Leontes' jealousy in his source for *WT*, Robert Greene's "Pandosto," in which the queen is visited in her bedchamber by the friend. (The incidents of bedchamber visiting in George Gascoigne's *The Adventures of Master F. J.* show both the innocence and the tinge of seduction associated with such behavior in Elizabethan society.) In making Leontes' jealousy less explicable, Shakespeare is moving toward the typical romantic plot opening.

The call is not universally to the bedroom, to battle, or to initiation. Joseph Campbell's monomyth, described in *The Hero with a Thousand Faces*, which primarily concerns romance (though Campbell does not distinguish among narrative types), uses initiation as a metaphor of all adventure. But the call of a romance is not universally to any one type of personal development, although it is always to the emergence and consolidation of identity. In *Childhood's End* the hero is the human race as a whole in its evolutionary development into a single mind; that demonstrates that the story is not always an individual's. Odysseus and Telemachus act independently in a single plot until the temporary binding unites them. Likewise, *WT* embraces two families and two generations in its process. Where there is a strong central figure, as is more generally true of romance, the fate of all is tied up in the fate of the one. Gilgamesh and Sir Gawain discover what they discover on behalf of all mankind; it will be up to Luke Skywalker and Frodo to save their worlds. Jung, in discovering his personal myth, provides a model of heroic individuation and advances consciousness in general. So does Siddhartha.

In the call, the characters are impelled into the plot by forces beyond their own volition. In the ordeal, the second stage of the plot, the teleological energy that erupted in the first stage makes itself felt in a seemingly random and confused way.

Stage 2. *The ordeal.*

"Allerleirauh": The girl's conditions are met by her father; she flees with her dresses and golden objects to hide in a hollow tree. *Beowulf:* (1)

Grendel consumes Danes, forbidding the tribe use of Heorot; (2) Grendel's mother kills Aeschere, again forbidding the Danes the use of their hall; (3) The dragon ravages Beowulf's land, burning his mead hall. *Childhood's End:* Stormgren is captured by men who wish independence from the Overlords and is rescued; the Overlords are seen to look like devils and their home planet is discovered. *Gilgamesh:* The prostitute civilizes Enkidu who, alienated from his home in the wild, goes in search of Gilgamesh. "Iron Hans": The hero enters the woods with Iron Hans, fails in his tasks, and is ejected with promises of aid from Iron Hans. "Knight's Tale": Palamon and Arcite free themselves from prison but not from Emily; therefore they remain in the land of their enemy. *LOTR:* The Companions of the Ring form and are endangered as they journey closer to the home of the enemy. *MDR:* Jung finds his proper career but his association with Freud proves unstable. *Odyssey:* Telemachus wanders; Odysseus tells his tales of hardship and adventure to the Phaiakians. *Siddhartha:* Siddhartha undertakes ascetic training as a forest sage but abandons that to seek Gautama. *Gawain:* Gawain, armed, wanders in search of the Green Knight. *Star Wars:* Luke, escaping various dangers (the Sand People, Imperial Stormtroopers, patrons of the Cantina), loses his home, is trained by Obi-Wan, and secures the aid of Han Solo. *WT:* Leontes' jealousy results in increasing disasters until he repents. *Wizard:* Ged is lured by Sarrat into casting a dangerous spell; he departs for the Wizard School on Roke.

Either the hero must leave home or, as with Leontes of *WT*, his home deserts him. Palamon and Arcite had already been taken from home, but before they were unwilling captives. Now they are driven to stay in a place dangerous to them. In *Childhood's End* the earth becomes a better place but something of a benign prison under the control of the Overlords.

Jung leaves a metaphorical home as Freud's successor in the psychoanalytic movement. Like the other romantic heroes, Jung was at a loss in the second stage of his plot as to his final direction. His career chose him as much as he chose it, at least in his experience. He is buffeted by the rude dangers of the world as is Odysseus, and like Odysseus he remains wary and resourceful enough to survive them.

In the ordeal stage, the dangers often take the form of forces that wish to retard the progress of the hero. In their most extreme form—Polyphemus the Cyclops, the garbage crusher on Darth Vader's Death Star, the monsters of Beowulf—the dangers threaten to consume the heroes. Circe, who wishes to keep Odysseus in the bedroom and out of the adventure, is a milder form of such a threat, as is Siddhartha's leader among the forest sages, whom he hypnotizes to escape. The same character may encourage development while seeming to retard it: Iron Hans, dangerous to other characters, is sympathetic to his captive boy and releases him although the boy bears the mark of the water that hid Iron Hans—it has turned his hair golden.

The hero is impelled to get on with the task of becoming more conscious. The assimilative threats that would impede that task might look at first glance female: the dark waters and caves of *LOTR*, the hungry mouths that often recall the Tooth Mother, eager to consume her child, to undo birth. But Iron Hans, a powerful figure who hides in the woods under water, is male, and he is both helper and captor of the male hero of the story; Enkidu's prostitute is the means by which he becomes conscious and so loses his place among animals, not the pull from consciousness represented by Circe, who turns men into animals. A retrograde pull will be there at this stage, and an impelling forward. The characters who push and pull the hero will often exhibit a sexual polarity, but their specific sexual orientation is not a modal characteristic.

A special mark of stage two in all modes is its confusion. The dangers seem to be coming at the hero from all sides and seem to have no principle of organization (although they often seem directional and organized in retrospect). The dangers may therefore multiply without violating any strong structural tugs other than the impulse to get on with the story. If we added five adventures for Odysseus at this stage (imported from Heliodorus's *Aethiopica*, the eighteenth century Chinese folk novel *Journey to the East*, the *Mahabharata*, or other romantic narratives that indulge in freely replicated dangers), the epic would accommodate them. Endless replication at this stage would create the perfect, ironized, inescapable romance. A redactor would have more difficulty adding episodes to the *Odyssey* once Odysseus reaches Ithaca. Past the temporary binding, romances take a firm direction.

The movement out of this stage toward the temporary binding, in retreat, is often manifested by a growing organization in the general situation of the hero. The constraint is sometimes physically expressed: Allerleirauh in her hollow tree, Luke Skywalker and his party in the garbage crusher, Gilgamesh and Enkidu or Palamon and Arcite locked in combat, the Companions of the Ring in the Mines of Moria. But sometimes, as in *Childhood's End*, the constraint is only a sense of a narrowing of choice, of a growing inevitability of conflict, or, as in *Gawain*, of desperation growing until Gawain seeks help in prayer. Leontes' jealous rage in *The Winter's Tale* does more and more damage—alienating the king's friend, killing his son and, as we think, his wife, sending his daughter and Paulina's husband off to die—so that finally Apollo condemns Leontes by oracle, and Leontes joins all those who stand aghast at what he has done.

Stage 3. *In retreat.*

"Allerleirauh": Discovered and mistaken for an animal, Allerleirauh is given a menial job in service to the king. *Beowulf:* (1) Beowulf arrives and discourses to the court before confronting Grendel; (2) Beowulf consoles Hrothgar before confronting Grendel's mother; (3) Beowulf discourses with his men before confronting the dragon. *Childhood's End:* New Athens is established as a utopia free from control by the Overlords. *Gilgamesh:* Gilgamesh and Enkidu unite in a friendship that defies the gods. "Iron Hans": The hero takes a position as an anonymous menial at the king's court. "Knight's Tale": Theseus proposes the tournament for Emily's hand. *LOTR:* Frodo offers the Ring to Galadriel in Lothlorien, center of positive ring power. *MDR:* Jung moves toward resolution of his confrontation with the unconscious in the dream of a golden island of light in the center of Liverpool. *Odyssey:* Odysseus returns to Ithaca and reunites with Telemachus. *Siddhartha:* Siddhartha sheds his identity and becomes a merchant in service to Kamala, the courtesan. *Gawain:* Gawain gains Bercilak's castle and makes his bargain to exchange winnings. *Star Wars:* Luke rescues Princess Leia and returns with her to the rebel base of her "father." (Obi-Wan Kenobi, slain by Darth Vader, is now manifested as a voice internal to Luke.) *WT:* Perdita is cynosure of the sheep-shearing festival. *Wizard:* Ged, most apt of pupils at the Wizard School, is taunted into evoking his shadow.

Something idyllic invests the temporary binding of a romance. Heroes often find themselves in a strange and attractive society in which they may have taken a disguise or have chosen to become anonymous. Perdita does not know who she is, nor Gawain where he is. Shakespeare's characters enter the Green World at this stage of his romances, just as the inventive people of *Childhood's End* build a utopia.

The characters usually believe that they have solved the problems that confronted them in the earlier stages of the plot. In every case the problem is larger than it seemed at first, and the difficulty announces itself here. Gawain believes that his greatest challenge is to find the castle of the Green Knight and that all that lies thereafter is to endure the stroke of the axe. The truth is that his test is just beginning. In *Childhood's End* the problem has seemed to be how to free people to achieve their potential under the reign of the Overlords, but beyond the temporary binding the human potential to become the Overmind will destroy traditional utopian solutions. Jung learns of the center of the Self but must carry that knowledge back to the world in which that Self came into existence and may pass away. Allerleirauh and the hero of "Iron Hans" have escaped their immediate problems and their families, but they are devalued and anonymous: their golden hair and beautiful clothing may be only glimpsed beneath the rags. Siddhartha will finally be almost swallowed by the merchant's identity he freely adopts. Palamon and Arcite have achieved the promise that one of them will marry Emily and are left with one another, and with mortality and the human condition in an ordered universe, as problems. Gilgamesh and Enkidu glory in their humanity but cannot escape its implication of mortality.

Beowulf believes that he goes to confront the forces that threaten the Danes and then the Geats. But the final dangers to those societies are internal. The mead hall of the Danes will fall not to monsters but to a feud among kin; the Danish dynasty is due for the same struggle between uncle and nephew as troubled the Swedes. Beowulf can fight monsters but not disloyal cowardice among his own men or the destructive feuds among kin. In the next plot stage the idylls of in retreat break down. The hero becomes passive as the transforming energy reaches its highest intensity. Disaster seems most imminent, but just as the most disorganized stage of labor immediately precedes birth, so transformation will follow.

Stage 4. *From the depths.*

"Allerleirauh": The heroine anonymously exhibits her self and her worth to the king, flees, and is pursued. *Beowulf:* (1) Beowulf waits in the darkness as Grendel eats Handscioh; (2) Beowulf is thrown to earth by Grendel's mother as his sword fails; (3) the dragon seizes Beowulf by the neck. *Childhood's End:* Jan stows away in the whale bound for the planet of the Overlords while the children of Earth transform; New Athens commits suicide. *Gilgamesh:* Enkidu dies; Gilgamesh, mourning, searches for the bounds of mortality and immortality. "Iron Hans": The hero is courted by the princess, who discovers the golden hair he hides; the hero in disguise helps the king. "Knight's Tale": Three deities give seemingly conflicting promises; the forces of Palamon and Arcite battle in the tournament. *LOTR:* Sam and Frodo journey into Mordor while Sauron's forces move to the attack on Gondor. *MDR:* Jung reports the ways in which his work was thrust upon him as a duty to the unconscious, his foreign travels, and his visions of death. *Odyssey:* Odysseus endures the suitors; his old nurse recognizes him and recalls his wound from the boar hunt; he enjoins her to secrecy. *Siddhartha:* The hero learns that he can become the merchant he despised and learns to love his unloving son. *Gawain:* Gawain fails the third test and receives a nick from the Green Knight. *Star Wars:* The Death Star threatens the rebel base; Han Solo intends to depart. *WT:* Perdita and Florizel flee the wrath of one father and run into trouble with the other. *Wizard:* After near disaster at the Court of the Terrenon, Ged ceases to flee the shadow and begins to pursue it.

Characters at the turn of plot stage four, from the depths, tend to have little control of their situation. Indeed, like Ged, Frodo, and Gilgamesh, they may succumb to unconsciousness. Looming threats, battles, and darkness reign. Jung, the utopians of *Childhood's End*, Allerleirauh, the hero of "Iron Hans," the lovers of *WT*, Ged, Gilgamesh, Siddhartha, and Frodo all resist the forces that are attempting to deliver them from their darkness; traces of resistance to deliverance show up in most romances (although not in *Beowulf*; the difference is surely culturally conditioned).

Even heroes like Odysseus and Beowulf are uncharacteristically passive. Odysseus must endure the taunts and missiles of the suitors; Beowulf lies supine while Grendel's mother hacks at his chest with a dagger. Gilgamesh cannot resist sleep. The heroes must sink beneath the surface of the baptismal waters before being reborn.

I do not mean to make Christian ritual the basic truth of romance but do intend to suggest that traditional symbolism gets close to the heart of the matter here. At this stage of the romantic plot of Spenser's *Fairy Queen*, book 1, the Red Cross Knight ascends to an upper room in the Castle of Alma to find that Charissa has just given birth. The new child is surely the Red Cross Knight himself, who has been reborn in charity. The gates that Galadriel's light must open in *LOTR* allow Sam to pass with Frodo, whom he has discovered unconscious from being beaten by orcs. Death and rebirth find the strongest structural suggestion at this point of romance (though, like any motif, rebirth may appear in other structural roles).

The teleological energy that has seemed so threatening in the ordeal stage of the plot, and here in from the depths seems about to do the hero in, proves finally to be the means of transformation. Only by momentarily succumbing, by lying back on the waters that carry him, can the hero achieve full identity.

Stage 5. *Identity*.

"Allerleirauh": The king recognizes Allerleirauh's full worth and marries her. *Beowulf:* (1) Beowulf mortally wounds Grendel and is praised; (2) Beowulf beheads Grendel's mother and returns to praise; (3) Beowulf kills the dragon, dies, and is buried with the treasure. *Childhood's End:* Humankind, save for the observer Jan, is transformed into the Overmind. *Gilgamesh:* Gilgamesh loses the plant of renewed youth. "Iron Hans": The princess reveals the boy's full identity; they marry. "Knight's Tale": Arcite dies; Palamon marries Emily. *LOTR:* Gollum, the Ring, and Frodo's finger disappear into Mt. Doom. *MDR:* Jung, a whole personality, reflects on death, the mind, and his place in the world. *Odyssey:* Odysseus, Telemachus, and their allies slay the suitors; Odysseus is reunited with Penelope and his father. *Siddhartha:* Govinda, kissing Siddhartha's forehead, perceives the Absolute. *Gawain:* Gawain learns the truth of his adventure and accepts the girdle as a token of his fault. *Star Wars:* Luke, guided by The Force, destroys the Death Star. *WT:* Perdita is recognized, Hermione revived. *Wizard:* Ged merges with his shadow.

The characters assume their full identity. Most of the works align the achieved identity of the characters with principles of universal order. Gawain defines an important feature of the human condition, our tendency to choose amiss. So do they all, each in its own way and in terms of the culture that produced the narrative.

At the end of a romance, characters emerge into the light of common day. That day may be celebrated, as it is in those plots that end with weddings (or, like *Siddhartha*, theophany), or it may be the mournful echo of Ragnarok at the end of *Beowulf*. The meditative moods of Gilgamesh, Jung, Frodo, and Chaucer's Theseus define a middle term. In all cases a common perception is that a magic has passed, for good and ill. The force that has called the characters to become what they have become vanishes from the world of the work. Where it has not, as in *Gawain* and *Star Wars*, further romances are promised. Morgan le Fay is not done with Arthur, nor Darth Vader with Luke.

The destruction of the Ring in *LOTR* means the end of both elves and orcs. The bittersweet quality that as Northrop Frye observes (1969, 37) characterizes romance arises from the essential identity of the destructive and creative, or retarding and furthering, potential of the teleological dynamic of romance. When Ged merges with his shadow, or when Gawain merges the gold of moral perfections with the green of his fleshly existence in the world, a holy marriage is consummated only a little less directly than in *WT*. Two great principles of opposition merge, resolving the tension that has generated the story. The world beyond the end of romance is the ordinary world of human choice.

The sixth stage of the plot, return, is missing in texts where the world in which the quest is completed is the same as the world of quotidian experience. Thus *Beowulf*, *MDR*, *Odyssey*, *Siddhartha*, *Star Wars*, *WT*, and *Wizard* lack the termination function. Certainly all the romances listed here achieve a firm closure. In all, some sort of rhetorical move signifying completion might be identified: in *Wizard* the promise of further adventures (the book is the first of a trilogy), in *Beowulf* the funereal cries and the final words of praise, in *MDR* Jung's final statement of a growing investment in the world and a correspondingly dwindling familiarity with his inner life. However, I choose to reserve the sixth stage process terminology for those works in which the heroes return, as Joseph Campbell says, the master of both worlds: the world in which the quest was completed, and the world of experience.

Stage 6. *Return.*

Childhood's End: The human race streams off to join the Overmind, consuming the earth as it goes. *Gilgamesh:* Gilgamesh returns to Uruk to resume his kingship. *LOTR:* Frodo sails from the Grey Havens; Sam returns to the cleansed Shire. *Gawain:* Gawain returns to court, where all adopt the green girdle.

None of the returns are purely celebrative. Frodo in his story and the human race in *Childhood's End* depart to unimaginable worlds of experience, states beyond death and life. When the conjunction of opposites at the conclusion of a romance is not celebrated as a *hieros gamos* where we are allowed to glimpse life past the conjunction, the world seems somewhat colorless compared to the drama just enacted.

Jung is the great psychological theorist of the romantic mode. The stages of analysis as described in the second of the *Two Essays on Analytical Psychology* (vol. 7) and elsewhere are roughly those of his individuation recorded in *Memories, Dreams, Reflections* and follow a romantic plot line as described in chapter 2. The effect of deep contact with the unconscious in the fourth stage, from the depths, is to leave the ego with an unstable overcharge of energy. This inflated state Jung calls the mana-personality (see *Two Essays*, 227–41). The main task at the resolution of an analysis is to place the energy back where it belongs: with the archetype of wholeness in the unconscious. The world, which had seemed full of the possibility of change because of the mana with which one confronted it, resumes its accustomed thereness, its opacity, power, and silence.

If Jung had left a case history as complete as that of the Wolf-Man, I would be tempted to analyze it here as a double to chapter 3. As it is I will let the brief indication of the structure of his autobiography stand in its place. I do hope I have at this point made clear the different universes from which Jung and Freud speak and the difference that makes in their analyses of experience.

Shakespeare's Romances

Many of Shakespeare's plays from *Comedy of Errors* on have secondary romantic plot lines. Six seem to me to have main plot lines in romance: *A Midsummer Night's Dream (MND)*, *As You Like It (AYL)*, *Pericles, Prince of Tyre (Per.)*, *Cymbeline (Cym.)*, *The Winter's Tale (WT)*, and *The Tempest (Tmp.)*. In my analysis of the entire group I show how the general plot snake allows generalizations about related works within a mode. The boundaries between the process stages must be somewhat arbitrary; the more definite demarcations are the changes of direction in the entropy curve. In almost every case the stages fall act by act, first process stage in the first act, fourth in the fourth, except for the sixth process stage, which is a luxury anyway, being an optional feature of the romance plot. The exceptions are the temporary binding of *Per.* and process stages two and three of *WT*. The suggestion is that the five-act structure has a powerful intuitive base. Perhaps we now know why Horace enjoined five acts for a drama in the *Ars Poetica*. The rule has had some success in the theatrical tradition for what I take to be adequate reasons.

The basic mystery is that while the five-act tradition dates from at least early Roman drama, plays have never had the four intermissions one would have expected if the acts were temporal units. Neither did a critical tradition ever develop that was truly adequate to account for the five-act division through plot theory. The history of the problem, however, has not lacked rationalizations, which often skirt what I take to be the truth.

Previous attempts to explain the five-act structure (notably in this century by T. W. Baldwin, who believed the divisions rational, and Henry L. Snuggs, who did not) generally suffer from an inadequate theory of plot structure. Baldwin finds that five acts were traditional in Roman theater and searches critical history to discover terms to describe the division. The general effect is to convince the reader that no consistent traditional terminology ever developed beyond essential agreement that plots have beginnings, middles, and ends. Since Aristotle's *Poetics*, all that theorists have done by way of elaboration is to insert a part between the beginning and the middle, and between the middle and the end, thus achieving five parts but not explaining why an essentially pyramidal structure needs five divisions rather than three, since the added parts are mere bridges.

I certainly thought about redefining traditional terms instead of attempting to freight the discussion with new ones. However, what I would gain in dignity and continuity within the tradition by using *epistasis* for *burnt fingers* and *catastasis* for *infernal vision* I might lose in clarity. In any case the traditional terms do not distinguish among different plot modes and do not bear meanings sufficiently close to the ones I need. The lack of modal distinctions (*comedy vs. tragedy* being a false trail, for reasons I will discuss in chapter 7), along with the dominance of Aristotle's metaphor in which a plot is like a knot that one ties and then unties, with its implied pyramidal structure, vitiated the development of an adequate traditional vocabulary. Aristotle's metaphor is just right enough to command attention, and just wrong enough to mislead. As I understand plot, the knot gets tied twice, once in the middle and once at the end, and the greatest unraveling occurs between the knots. But we are no longer talking about string, and the metaphor breaks down.

One objection to the traditional terms I do not share is that of Marco Mincoff, who believes that historical changes have made the terms that were applicable to Roman comedy inapplicable to Elizabethan (1965, 932). The traditional terms are as clumsy for one as for the other.

Baldwin does pull together comments from the tradition of plot analysis that seem to me to be on the way to illuminations. He quotes, for example, Christopher Landino, who in his 1482 edition of Horace explained that "the matter is so divided into five that the first part unfolds the argument. The second seeks to bring to an end the things which already have been begun. The third brings on perturbation and the impediments and despair of the desired thing. The fourth brings a remedy for the impending evil. The fifth brings the whole to the desired outcome" (1947, 112). A real perception is trying to break through this confused language: that the second and fourth parts are not in a straight line with the first, third, or fifth. The insight, however, remains undeveloped.

The most naively hopeful modern attempt to rationalize five-act structure is W. H. Fleming's *Shakespeare's Plots* (1902). In a heavily prescriptive application of the idea that since life has five stages ("birth, rise, culmination, decline, and fall"), so should every decent play, Fleming does his best to push and pull Shakespeare's plays into their proper shape (1902, 29). Where the plays will simply not fit, he pushes and pulls on his terminology (which he derives from a creative reading of Aristotle). The Procrustean archetype has possessed him, and his book is a great caution to anyone who would attempt the structural analysis of plot. It could serve as the shadow of this book.

Emrys Jones summarizes responsible modern discussion of the five-act problem in *Scenic Form in Shakespeare* (1971). He believes that Shakespeare may have had a five-part structure vaguely in mind "as a kind of clock so that the allocation of time to the various parts of his material would be proportionate, and yet doing so in such a free and unsystematic way that the finished play does not very obviously suggest five clearly marked stages" (1971, 68). One can hardly argue that the stages are clearly marked when so few have observed any rationale for them.

Perhaps we have not had the stages of plot worked out long ago because we were not yet ready to be that conscious of the true status of our narratives. We had not stepped far enough outside them to see their shape, although we long ago stepped outside myth. As I said in connection with my analysis of *She Stoops to Conquer*, I do not find it easy to analyze the plot of any but the simplest texts. I hope the reader will read the following analyses patiently with as full a memory of the plays as can be mustered.

Stage 1. *The call.*

In Shakespeare, *characters are denied their natural roles in the family and in society by older male family heads.* The prohibitions have about them something dark—something irrational and compulsive. Because the disruptive energy is teleological, its emergence in the obstructive males is weakly motivated. The call is only expressing itself *through* the irrational jealousies and desires; they themselves do not furnish the impetus of the plot but only the evidence of that impetus. Characters have the sense of suffering from some inexplicable disaster.

MND to 1.1.46. The first plot turn comes when Egeus attempts to force Hermia's marriage. The theme of sexual prohibition has already appeared with Theseus and Hippolyta, but there as a willing restraint.

AYL to 1.1.23. The first turn comes almost immediately with the struggle of Orlando and his brother Oliver. Two sets of brothers will prove to be locked in hostility, and Rosalind and Celia will flee their uncle and father, Ferdinand. Charles the wrestler will badly wound three brothers before Orlando defeats him, thus accomplishing intrafamilial damage if not intrafamilial hostility. Familial hostility spreads throughout the play in the first two plot stages.

Per. to 1.1.56. Pericles, not knowing that Antiochus and his daughter are in an incestuous union, tries to win her in a rigged riddle game. The turn comes with his discovery of the incest. The resolution of this plot comes only when Pericles is able to express proper love for his daughter, which occurs only after she has maintained chastity in the most lascivious environment. While Pericles has never expressed *im*proper love for his daughter, such love has been expressed in the play. It is present and must be dealt with. Thus Antiochus's desire for his daughter may be said to initiate the teleological energy that drives the plot, although he appears on stage only here.

Cym. to 1.1.70. Cymbeline intervenes in his daughter's marriage by banishing her husband, Posthumus, in the turn of the first stage. Later Cymbeline himself will wonder at his susceptibility to the evil influence of his wife, by whose will he acts.

WT to 1.2.120. Leontes is possessed by jealousy in 1.2.

Tmp. to 1.2.187. The turn comes with the shipwreck of the court party. The play is unusual in that the teleological energy is largely under the control of Prospero. While he must cooperate (as must all magicians in his tradition) with "a most auspicious star" (1.2.182), yet he shapes the plot, and the revelations of identity that are the business of the play are contrived by him. It is no wonder if he sometimes speaks, as in the revels passage, with providential authority.

Stage 2. *The ordeal.*

In Shakespeare, *victims (characters denied their natural roles) flee (or are banished by) the machinations of close relatives.* The ordeals all involve some degree of loss of identity. In the mildest form of identity loss, the characters are among strangers and may be freed from the usual social constraints on their behavior (as in the Green World); at the extreme is Hermione in *WT*, who is thought dead, appears to Antigonus as if from beyond the grave (3.3.15–38), and retires entirely from the action until the end of the play.

MND to 2.1.46. The four lovers flee into the forest; Titania and Oberon quarrel. The turn comes when Oberon secures the herb that will lead to the enchantments of the temporary binding (2.1).

AYL to 2.4. Rosalind flees to Arden to escape Duke Frederick, and

Orlando to escape him and Oliver. Orlando's flight in 2.3 is the turn of this second stage. The turn does not come with Rosalind's earlier flight because uniquely with Orlando's flight a temporary binding becomes possible.

Per. to 2.2. Pericles guesses the riddle, flees the murderous father Antiochus, and is shipwrecked. The shipwreck, 2.1, is the turn to the temporary binding; until that point he has been the object of increasingly destructive misfortunes. Now anonymous, he begins to remake his fortunes.

Cym. to 3.3. Imogen, victimized by her father, Cloten, and Iachimo, flees to Milford Haven to meet (she believes) her banished husband. Iachimo's invasion of Imogen's bedchamber in 2.2 provides the turn. It is the depth of Imogen's victimization, heavy with the imagery of rape. What Iachimo sees provides him with the false evidence of Imogen's supposed infidelity he needs to deceive Posthumus and thus leads to the temporary binding.

WT to 3.3. Polixenes flees his old friend Leontes; the victimized Hermione reportedly dies, and her daughter is banished to be exposed. Apollo's prophecy is the turn of the plot curve. While the prophecy itself occurs in 3.2, the messengers bearing it are announced at the end of act 2, and the prophecy could be taken as bridging the acts. Or one could note an anomalous mismatch of process turn and act.

Tmp. to 3.1. The shipwrecked Ferdinand is led to Miranda and falls under the direct control of her father, as does the court party. Caliban finds a new master. The turn comes at 2.1 when Prospero (through Ariel) defeats the assassination attempt on Alonso. The attempt is a low point of villainy, and Prospero's benevolent intervention moves the plot in a new direction.

Stage 3. *In retreat.*

In Shakespeare, *nonce societies are established about the fugitives, who assume artificial and contrived roles.* The loss of identity suffered in the previous action has made it possible for important characters to try on new roles, new ways of behaving. The process stage features a strong sense of the idyll—even if the idyll is violated (*Tmp.*) or a parody (*MND*).

MND to 3.2.345. Titania falls in love with the transformed Bottom. The lovers are enchanted and pursue one another. Bottom's transformation in 3.1 is the turn. Unrestrained love is achieved, but the object of unrestrained love becomes a beast, the love bestial. (More, of course, is signified than I can imagine being able to say; I intend to indicate only the rationale for my presentation of the plot, here and elsewhere.)

AYL to 4.1. Rosalind, in disguise, is wooed by Orlando, as is Audrey by

Touchstone and Phebe by Silvius. The turn comes in 3.2 as Rosalind and Orlando meet in Arden. Orlando is able to speak of his love, but only to Ganymede as if to Rosalind, in an indirection similar to those practiced by Allerleirauh, Cinderella, the hero of "Iron Hans," and the Grimms' heroine, the Goose Girl. Touchstone's wooing of Audrey parodies the main relationship in one direction, that of Silvius and Phebe in the opposite. Both parodies represent tendencies of the relationship between Orlando and Rosalind. Like the play of Pyramus and Thisbe in *MND*, the parodic relationships are shadows, possibilities inherent in the situation. Orlando is almost as moony as Silvius in his poems-on-trees stage, and Rosalind's tongue has sometimes almost the tang of Touchstone's. Jaques's role is analogous. His peculiar blend of mourning, sentimentality, and mockery completes a tendency in the relationship of Rosalind and Orlando. Jaques is the unredeemed one who would not choose to leave Arden.

Per. to 3.2. Pericles, anonymous in his father's rusty armor, wins Simonides' daughter and then loses her at sea. Pericles' winning of Thaisa at the end of act 2 is the turn; the beginning of act 3 opens the movement toward the infernal vision. Again, the turn comes at the juncture of acts.

Cym. to 4.1. Imogen discovers her husband's murderous intent and finds refuge as Fidele with Belarius and the brothers in the Welsh cave. The turn comes as Imogen joins her brothers and Belarius in 3.6. She can now be prized at something like her true worth, although not in her true identity. The same might be said of the other main characters of Shakespearean romance at this stage.

WT to 4.4.410. Perdita is the cynosure of the sheep-shearing festival in Bohemia. The turn comes in 4.4 as Florizel and Perdita stand at the center of the pastoral festival; Polixenes provides the movement downwards under his son's provocation. This turn is an anomaly in coming in the fourth act but not at all anomalous otherwise. My only conclusion is that the rationale for a five-act structure is not so psychologically compelling as to forestall misfits.

Tmp. to 3.3.53. Ferdinand accepts his role as wood gatherer; Caliban and party plot an insurrection; the court party is led to a banquet. The turn comes at 3.1 with Ferdinand and Miranda's mutual profession of love. In all the romances a love, nurtured in seclusion and anonymity, provides the center on which the plot turns. (In *Cym.*, the love is that between Imogen and her brothers.) *Tmp.* lays great stress on chastity, as does *Per.*; the restraint that Prospero enjoins on Miranda and Ferdinand is necessary to a just and humane society. Without the strictures we place on ourselves, the rules of civility collapse into those of the societies projected by the belly-cheer group with Caliban or the Machiavels with Alonso, perversions of the appetite and the reason. *MND*, in contrast, invokes restraint through negative example and is not open to the reading in which the rules of restraint are human conventions instead of universal principles. *Tmp.* shares with the other late plays a sense of the necessity of human artifice (and, most notably in *King Lear*, the possibility of its failure).

Stage 4. *From the depths.*

In Shakespeare, *characters fall into the hands of threatening but ultimately benevolent characters (or of a train of events of a similar nature) who destroy their nonce relationships and move them back toward the family unit.* Characters often succumb to sleep or to seeming death while forces are operating for their deliverance.

MND to 4.1.102. The disenchantment of almost everyone in 4.1 provides the turn. The mounting confusions are at that point allayed; the human lovers had been reduced to wandering in the darkness, following the illusory voices of Puck.

AYL to 5.4. Phebe falls in love with Rosalind, thinking her to be a man. Oliver's report of his rescue from the hungry lioness and the snake in 4.3 is the plot turn. The fraternal hostility that initiated the plot is confronted with the healing experience of Arden. The lioness and the snake that Orlando conquers are partially in himself. He is now able to spurn them even as Titania rejects Bottom or Marina her customers. The lioness and snake can be said to express a range of qualities from wrath and envy to the maternal hostility of a tooth mother and homosexuality (the snake is darting into Oliver's mouth); I find it useful to think of them as unworthy manifestations of eros, creative energy perverted into fraternal aggression.

Per. to 5. Marina's virtue is proof against the brothel in 4.6, the fourth plot turn. Pericles has been able to express appropriate affection in the third stage (his wooing of and marriage to Thaisa); so have the other heroes and heroines of these romances. In the fourth process stage, they must assert the ability to govern their affections or recognize the implications of ungoverned eros. Until Marina has exercised virtue, Thaisa cannot be released from Diana nor Pericles from melancholy. In Marina is undone what Antiochus's daughter has begun.

Cym. to 5.5. Imogen's "death" in 4.2, followed by her confrontation with Cloten's headless corpse (which she takes to be that of Posthumus), provides the turn. From this point the salvation of Britain begins, and the virtue represented by Imogen, her brothers, and Belarius moves back toward the court, saving even the woefully faulty Posthumus.

WT to 5.2. Polixenes threatens his son and Perdita. The plot turns about Camillo's plan in 4.4 to lead the lovers to Leontes' court and thus to discovery.

Tmp. to 5.1. The masque of Ceres in 4.1, the turn, asserts abundance without ungoverned appetite (Venus and Cupid are not in attendance). The paradoxical dance of nymphs and reapers with which the masque closes, a dance of spring and autumn, life and death, finds echoes in the other plays. In this fourth stage, as the characters have almost succumbed to distraction, death, or death's simulacrum, sleep, they are delivered either by their own virtue or by the kindness of others. In this case, Prospero simply recalls his situation (Caliban and his party are approaching with murderous intent), shows us the void beneath our feet, and proceeds to deal with the threat.

Stage 5. *Identity.*

In Shakespeare, *all characters find their appropriate social and familiar roles, assuming their full worth and dignity.* The achieved wholeness is expressed in appropriate marital and familial relationships.

MND to end. The turn comes in 5.1 as the couples, awaiting their appropriate unions, witness the disastrous results of inappropriate union in the story of Pyramus and Thisbe. The pain is so distanced by its comic presentation as not to disrupt the celebratory atmosphere.

AYL to 5.4.145. Hymen joins the couples in marriage.

Per. to 5.3.77. The turn comes in 5.1 when Marina and Pericles are reunited. The reunion with Thaisa flows as a consequence.

Cym. to end. Cymbeline recognizes his daughter, and Posthumus his wife, in 5.2, the turn.

WT to end. Perdita's recognition occurs offstage to allow Hermione's revival in 5.3 to form the turn.

Tmp. to 5.1.306. The discovery of Ferdinand and Miranda in 5.1 provides the turn. Prospero has not lost his daughter in the sense that Alonso understands (5.1.148), but he has finally both lost and found her just as do all the other fathers in this stage of the Shakespearean romance.

Stage 6. *Return.*

Where identity has not been achieved in the world of experience, the characters return, bringing with them a justified society.

MND (missing)

AYL Duke Frederick's conversion is the turn; the court party (save for Jaques) departs Arden.

Per. Simonides' death permits Pericles and Thaisa to succeed him, and Lysimachus and Marina to succeed Pericles in Tyre.

Cym. (missing)

WT (missing)

Tmp. Prospero proposes to return to Italy and releases Ariel. His supplanting of his brother is structurally similar to Simonides' death and Frederick's conversion.

Of all Shakespeare's romances, *As You Like It* has generated the most modally based confusion. In his New Penguin edition of the play (Shakespeare, 1968), H. J. Oliver prints this stage direction following 5.4.101: "*Enter a masquer representing Hymen, and Rosalind and Celia as themselves. Still music.*" But the copy text (and only contemporary authority) has instead "*Enter Hymen, Rosalind, and Celia. Still music.*" In his preface and notes Oliver explains that Hymen's entrance must surely be a masque, like the ones in *Cym.* and *Timon of Athens.* But Posthumus's dream in *Cym.* 5.4 is not a masque, and the masque of Cupid in *Tim.* 1.2, an actual masque, is announced as one expects masques to be announced. Both Posthumus's dream and the masque of Cupid are set off from the consensual reality on stage. Within the consensual reality of *AYL*, Hymen is almost as real as Rosalind. He receives no special announcement as an entertainment, nor is he an apparition. Hymen simply joins the scene unquestioned by the other characters. He even makes a joke about Touchstone and Audrey: "You and you are sure together / As the winter to foul weather" (5.4.129–30). His short lines and prominent rhymes do distinguish him from the others on stage and place him in the company of other theophanic appearances—Posthumus's vision in *Cym.*, the masque of Ceres in *Tmp.*, Diana's appearance to Pericles—yet none have quite Hymen's status on stage as full character. His impact can be quite strong. I will admit that even on television, in the BBC *Shakespeare Plays* production, Hymen's entrance over the hill brought tears to my eyes. His entrance seemed too good to be true and yet was true, a grace-affirming providence.

Why, then, would Oliver feel so sure of Hymen's artificiality as to indicate it in a stage direction? In romance, the marriages at the end represent a kind of hieros gamos, a celebration of the union of opposites, a wholeness achieved in the single psychic system that embraces all characters and all actions of the fiction. The god of marriage might well attend such a union. Why would Kenneth Muir dismiss Hymen altogether as somehow not a serious theophany (Tobias and Zolbrod 1974, 32) in an article that supports Oliver's stage direction? Perhaps because, in Oliver's and Muir's experience of the play, the organization of the fictive universe is such that gods do not appear to celebrate marriages. For the critic and the editor, Rosalind has taken care of herself and does not require divine presentation except as a device to save her from appearing forward. But from such a point of view, the play appears more faulty than I have indicated in my analysis above. Harold Jenkins does find it so, in an article that has been widely quoted.

> It is in the defectiveness of its action that *As You Like It* differs from the rest of the major comedies—in its dearth not only of big theatrical scenes but of events linked together by the logical intricacies of cause and effect. Of comedy, as of tragedy, action is the first essential; but *As You Like It* suggests that action is not, if I may adapt a phrase of Marston's, "the life of these things." It may be merely the foundation on which they are built. And *As You Like It* further shows that on a very flimsy foundation, if only you are skilful enough, a very elaborate structure may be poised. But the method has its dangers, and though Shakespeare's skill conceals these dangers from us, *Twelfth Night*, as I said, returns to a more orthodox scheme. (1955, 41)

The "logical intricacies of cause and effect" that Jenkins has in mind are surely those of the low mimetic universe of the main plot of plays such as *Twelfth Night*. (The text with which Oliver most closely associates *AYL* is *Two Gentlemen of Verona*, another play with a main plot line in low mimesis.) The effect of treating *AYL* as primarily low mimetic is to make much of the play seem careless and some of the action inexplicable. In a romantic report of the play (but not in Jenkins's or Oliver's) Hymen's entrance is big and theatrical enough. In an experience of the play as romance, many scenes will take on a numen that they lack in the low mimetic dimension, for in low mimesis meaning arises from human intention. Motivation is primary in low mimesis, secondary in romance, where the characters act within the stream of teleological purpose. David Young observes in *The Heart's Forest* that Fortune, not individual will, guides the action of the play (1972, 42). His observation is consistent with the romantic plot but not with the low mimetic. As plot is an experience of a process of change, the play will yield both plots, contradictory though the experiences are.

In romance, Rosalind's disguise as Ganymede is necessary to the reformation of her identity. It is a feature of her retreat, from which she will be delivered by Hymen, and out of which she continually peeps even as does Allerleirauh. But in the secondary low mimetic plot line, her disguise alters. As Jenkins sees it,

> By the time we reach the second act Rosalind has already come safe to the Forest of Arden, by the aid of her man's disguise. From this disguise, as everybody knows, springs the principal comic situation of the play. But such is the inconsequential nature of the action that this comic situation develops only when the practical need for the disguise is past. (1955, 41)

To Jenkins, the disguise is pointless. But it is so only in the low mimetic dimension of the play. From that viewpoint, not only does the use of disguise seem trivial, but so does the pastoralism of the play in general.

I will add one example of antipastoral criticism to stand for pages of objections by other critics to the lioness and palm tree of Arden, Oliver's conversion, the pastimes of the Duke and his company, and the pastoral tradition in general. E. C. Pettet discusses *AYL* in the chapter "Shakespeare's Detachment from Romance" of his *Shakespeare and the Romance Tradition* (1970):

> Shakespeare revealed the pastoral, critically, for what it really was—a precious and high artificial form of writing and a fashionable mode of escapism from the court-life of the time, which most courtiers of sensibility and intelligence discovered from experience to be more sordid, exhausting and dangerous than it appeared from a distance. (1970, 131)

The play will support such hardheaded statements, but not as a romance. The realism that Pettet attributes to experienced Elizabethan courtiers is low mimetic realism, not romantic realism. In romance the hard fact, discoverable by experience, is that the pastoral atmosphere of Arden provides an appropriate context for a movement toward emergent identity. True, Shakespeare's presentation of the tradition in the play is full of the oppositions of paradox, but in a romantic reading the center of the paradoxes lies within the pastoral tradition. (See David Young's chapter on pastoral tradition and *AYL* for a sensitive discussion of this issue.)

In the same company of the low mimetic vision of the play belong readings that overprize Touchstone or Jaques, or that reduce Rosalind's opinions on love to her wry aphorism: "Men have died from time to time, and worms have eaten them, but not for love" (4.1.96–98). All such misprisions of the experience of the play as romance infect discussions that emphasize the experience of its secondary low mimetic plot. But a description of the low mimetic plot line will account for less of the experience of the play than will a description of the romantic plot line. The play seems more defective when experienced as primarily low mimetic than as primarily romantic. For that reason I consider that the main plot line is romantic. And for analogous reasons, I consider that the main plot lines of *Twelfth Night* and *The Merchant of Venice* are low mimetic, although their strong secondary romantic plot lines would allow meaningful comparisons with the romances.

The low mimetic plot line of *AYL* has much the same shape as the romantic plot line. The quarrel of brothers still initiates the plot, which is driven by Oliver's desire to gain his proper status. (His desire is shared by Rosalind and the others associated with the deposed Duke.) The social blunders stage emphasizes the friendship of Celia and Rosalind, Orlando's bashful reaction to Rosalind, and the kindness of Celia and Adam. The simple solutions phase finds Orlando and Rosalind courting, which solves Orlando's problem since he has found a relationship with a possible mate of suitable social station, but the solution is temporary because she is in disguise (inexplicably, in this plot line). The other actions occurring in Arden—songs, wooings, encounters, encomia, and disquisitions—seem fragments in this plot line because the characters are perceived as being essentially independent in low mimesis, and because so much of the action is unrelated to the main business of getting on with the marriage and the regaining of social station. Not much seems to happen between the time the lovers enter Arden and the time they leave. The isolation stage of the low mimetic plot is therefore weak. What isolation exists is voluntary, like Jaques', or is a result of Rosalind's disguise, like the isolation of Orlando and of Silvius. In the firm society final binding, Duke Frederick's conversion seems mere contrivance. Hymen is there mostly to indicate that the time is at hand for marriages and for the characters to assume appropriate social stations. Recounted exclusively in low mimesis, "the mere story of the play is relatively unimportant" (Shakespeare 1968, 8–9). Howard Felperin remarks that "all that Duke Senior need do to regain his dukedom is wait for his wicked brother to follow him into the forest, where he undergoes a religious conversion" (1972, 59), and later adds that "this could have been accomplished in the first act" (1972, 70). We will value the play because Shakespeare "retained, and enhanced, the charming artifice of his original and at the same time smilingly revealed its conventionality and unreality" (Shakespeare 1968, 11). But we will miss the way in which the play seriously enacts a celebration of identity within the reality of romance.

Many critics have written from their experience of the play as a romance—I have mentioned David Young and should add Douglas Peterson's valuable study *Time, Tide, and Tempest* and Theresa Coletti's pairing of *AYL* and *Tmp.* in "Music and *The Tempest*" (Tobias and Zolrod 1974, 185–99). Yet for some reason the more usual thing is to see the play as a strange cousin of the low mimetic comedies. Perhaps the answer lies in our sense of Shakespeare's dramatic development, arising from the usual order in which the plays are printed, and from our sense of the order of their composition. We are led to pair *AYL* with comedies that have a primary plot in low mimesis but a strong secondary romantic plot, plays like *Much Ado About Nothing* and *Twelfth Night* that share many motifs with *AYL*. The juxtaposition skews our remembrance of the play. What is more, the critical tradition will condition our experience if we are aware of it. If we think that we know that the play is a slight and affectionate exposé of pastoral tradition, we are more likely to fasten on that potential within our experience of the play.

My understanding is that our experience (before we attempt to articulate it) is a single system of understandings and impressions, many of them in conflict. When we try to articulate our experience, we naturally elicit consistency. In the primary critical tradition concerning *AYL*, the consistency has been that of low mimetic reality assumptions.

Northrop Frye in *The Secular Scripture* seems to have the low mimetic plot line in mind when he sees *AYL* as "more comedy than romance" (1976, 150), using a distinction between romance and comedy developed in "The Structure and Spirit of Comedy." I am a little embarrassed to say that I do not find useful this application of his terminology, which I have appropriated. I believe that inadequate definition has been responsible for much loose usage of modal terms, and do not wish to be held accountable for discussions at variance with my own use of them, even when the writer is someone I found as inspiring as Northrop Frye. I see no exclusivity in the terms *romance* and *comedy*. Modal distinctions are fundamental. Comedy and tragedy are features of plots within literary universes and do not themselves constitute exclusive universes.

The experience of *AYL* in low mimesis must be possible and legitimate, for so many intelligent persons of good will have experienced the play in that way. I hope that my plot analysis above, and my comments on romance, are sufficient to convey an experience of the play as a romance. We must, then, finally recognize both experiences. I believe that when I attend to the play well both experiences are simultaneous. When I try to speak of the play, one becomes dominant. In terms of the rabbitduck (fig. 3), I must perceive the possibility of both patterns, or I would be able to hold one firmly in mind and ignore the other. But once I have seen a valid presentation of two plot lines or have become conscious of two dimensions of my experience, I will no longer be wedded to absolute judgments based on modal blinders. However, if I suspect that my sense of consistency is threatened but am not yet really conscious of the alternative modal formulation, I may expend a great deal of energy to maintain a single vision. From that energy arises much heat in scholarly discussion. My point, then, is not that the experience of *AYL* in low mimesis is wrong. My point is that a more comprehensive discussion of the play, one in which more of the experience is made conscious, will be aware of both plot lines and will recognize that the romantic plot line dominates.

Three of Shakespeare's romances share a particularly close congruity of plot. Plot analysis allows one to talk about *Per.*, *Cym.*, and *WT* at the same time in such a way as to elicit their common process in some detail.

In the initiation stage, the call, secret sexual liaisons, real or imagined, threaten normal family relationships. Jealously possessive fathers are the immediate source of threat; they attempt to prevent the females from enjoying normal and warm relationships. Mothers are compromised: they are replaced either by a daughter unnaturally (*Per.*) or by a scheming stepmother (*Cym.*), or they are under suspicion (*WT*). A man from outside the family is threatened by the father: a suitor (*Per.*), a new husband (*Cym.*), or a friend from youth (*WT*). Each play features a highly desirable woman in the call: Antiochus's daughter, Imogen, and Hermione. The action is initiated by an ungovernable abundance of eros, visited on the characters as if from outside and expressed by the fathers as unreasoning hostility.

In the burnt fingers stage, the ordeal, parental would-be poisoners send subordinates to spread venom. In *Per.*, the poisoner cannot find Pericles; in *Cym.*, the doctor substitutes a soporific for the poison; in *WT*, Camillo warns Polixenes. Suitors, real or imagined (*WT*), are forced to flee. Kings have real trouble governing: Pericles, Cymbeline, and Leontes are all becoming impotent in their kingdoms. The courts are driven into seeming and hypocrisy by the jealous rage of the king-fathers Antiochus, Cymbeline, and Leontes. The primary sympathetic character is reduced to a helpless victim: Pericles, shipwrecked and alone, craves death; Imogen lies sleeping under Iachimo's treacherous eyes; Hermione languishes vilified in prison. At the end of this process stage, paternalistic wrath has succeeded in (disastrously) wiping out the old tensions and dangers: Leontes has had his empty triumph over Hermione; Posthumus believes that he has proved Imogen to be a whore; Fortune and Antiochus have stripped the fugitive Pericles of power, friends, and identity.

In the tentative binding, or in retreat, stage in all three plays, something of a fresh start is made, out of reach of the now impotent and formerly wrathful males. Pericles, Imogen, and Perdita become cynosures of societies isolated from the previous worlds of the plays. The plays share the following structure at this stage: (1) a loss of identity in flight or banishment and (2) an idyll. Pericles becomes the Rusty Knight; the fugitive Imogen learns of Posthumus' order that she be murdered and takes on man's clothing as Fidele; Perdita is abandoned as an infant in Bohemia. All are unrecognized or in disguise.

All the idylls begin with a challenge by males. Pericles takes on all challengers and becomes both center of attention and suitor of Thaisa. Imogen as Fidele is a marvel to her unrecognized brothers in the Welsh cave. Perdita answers Polixenes satisfactorily as the hostess of the sheep-shearing festival. The girls are admired for their intrinsic charm and for their domestic skills, Pericles for his martial ability. All represent the persistence of sexual identity under threat and beyond the roles these characters would normally play in society. All are objects of great and spontaneous affection. In fact, the affection threatens to go beyond bounds. Belarius says that he would court Fidele if "he" were a girl; Perdita acts to moderate the bawdy tendencies at the festival; Simonides becomes joshingly threatening toward Pericles.

In the Infernal Vision, from the depths, stage, the plays share a substructure in which (1) the idyll is shattered and (2) the fathers and husbands reenter the play. The idyll is shattered as motifs of grisly death and mourning appear—Thaisa's death at sea and Leonine's intention to murder Marina, the mourning of Fidele and her own mourning over Cloten's headless body, and Autolycus's description of the baroque deaths in store for the shepherd and his son. The threatened females—Marina, Imogen, and Perdita—are passive at this point. The breaking of the idyll entails a certain amount of sexual frustration or isolation. Marina, having talked Lysimachus out of seduction and Boult out of rape, becomes the leader of a group of maidens. Her mother has elsewhere joined the maidens serving Diana. Imogen believes that the beheaded would-be rapist Cloten is her husband. Perdita believes that her courtship with Florizel is over. In all three plays an immediate breaker of the idyll is a close but not a blood kin: Dionyza the foster mother, Cloten the step-brother, and Polixenes the prospective father-in-law (assuming Perdita as the focus of interest, as she temporarily is). The threats are no longer directly sexual as they were at the beginning of the plays, nor do they issue from so close a source.

The fathers and husbands reenter the play now repentant and mournful—in fact, close to suicidal. Pericles seems to be succumbing to a fatal melancholy because he believes his wife and daughter dead. Posthumus joins battle in order to be killed and seeks death as a prisoner to atone for the murder (as he believes) of his wife. Leontes welcomes the salt that Paulina rubs into his memories of Hermione. The eros that drove the men in the earlier parts of the plays now rests almost entirely with the daughter-wives, by whom it will again be aroused in the father-husbands, but this time in proper measure.

In the final binding, or identity, stage, the plays' common substructure includes (1) recognition, (2) restored wives, and (3) reconciliation. Daughters in disguise are darkly recognized by their deeply moved fathers. All three fathers—Pericles, Cymbeline, and Leontes—have reached a condition of impotent withdrawal (Cymbeline's the least extreme). The presence of their yet unrecognized daughters leads them to admiration. The daughters are then fully recognized.

Close to the point at which wives are restored the plays share a motif of divine visitation, if Paulina's magic may be so called. All three marvels—Pericles' vision of Diana, Posthumus's vision of his ancestors and of Jupiter, and Paulina's revival of Hermione's statue—result in the restoration of a wife. In all cases is implied an element of divine decision that the conditions for restoration have been satisfied. The primary condition is that the fathers recognize and embrace their daughters. Once the feminine presence has been properly recognized in the daughters, it may be joined through union with the wives. In *Cym.* the evil queen (a stepmother) dies, and Imogen plays roles of both wife and daughter. *Per.* seems at first anomalous in having a male at the focus, but while the sexual polarities of the plot are reversed for *Per.* in the temporary binding, that play, too, is a story of the loss and re-emergence of the feminine.

With the parents removed from their frozen sorrow and at least one couple reunited in each play as the center of a family unit, the several kings resume or begin an orderly reign. In all three plays oracles have been fulfilled (oracles in *Per.* by Diana; in *Cym.* by Jupiter and through birdflight; in *WT* by Apollo). The final bindings of the plays thus suggest that a cosmic justice has been fulfilled, a universal design completed. Peace is established between formerly hostile kingdoms. In *Per.*, the hostile Cleon and Dionyza are dead at the hands of their own citizens and the pseudo-hostile Simonides by causes undeclared; in *Cym.*, Britain and Rome are reunited, as are Bohemia and Sicilia in *WT*.

A Generic Map of Romance

"Allerleirauh" shares features with Shakespearean romance that go beyond common motifs to a similarity in the types of energies that their plots bind. Allerleirauh's father's excessive and threatening eros drives her into retreat and from her accustomed identity until she can be recognized through a process of partial revelations by her proper husband and can herself be the source and object of properly directed eros. The same may be said of the main characters in Shakespeare's romances. Surely the romance of eros is an easily identifiable genre. It is defined by specific identity of the teleological energy that drives the plot. That energy determines the form of identity that the heroes achieve. Generic definitions that hope to identify similarities among plots within a mode—that is, among processes implying a common causal modality—can find no more fundamental discriminant than energy type.

For an approach to the genres of romance that will serve to associate the romances analyzed in this chapter with their appropriate fellows, one could begin by distinguishing those romances in which relationships with others are primary from those that are preoccupied with internal states. Romances of eros turn outside the hero to link him or her to others. Erotic romances among those outlined in this chapter include the Shakespearean romances, "Allerleirauh," "Iron Hans," "The Knight's Tale," *The Odyssey*, and *Star Wars*.

The romances of eros fall into two groups. The more capacious group is the romance of regained unity. Its subgroup is the romance of initiation.

Shakespeare's romances, *The Odyssey*, and Chaucer's "Knight's Tale" share a pattern of regained family unity. A little generalization of the broader plot scheme for Shakespeare's romances would allow one to talk about the *Odyssey* and "The Knight's Tale" at the same time. The major difference in Homer is that the dangers of *The Odyssey* come not from the father (although his desires are misdirected at the beginning) but from his would-be replacers, the suitors, and from Poseidon, himself the wronged father of Polyphemus. "The Knight's Tale," like *Midsummer Night's Dream* and *As You Like It*, concerns mostly the young lovers but begins and ends in the context of the larger, reestablished society.

Romances of initiation such as "Allerleirauh," "Iron Hans," and *Star*

Wars tell the stories of young people establishing themselves in adult roles. The romance of regained identity subsumes the romance of initiation: initiation is a space within the larger territory of regained unity. From the point of view of regained unity, as at the end of *The Odyssey* or *The Winter's Tale*, the romance of initiation takes one only past adolescence. Orlando and Rosalind are going through an initiation into adulthood within a larger movement toward an instauration lightly suggested in their play, as in *Midsummer Night's Dream*, but prominent in the later Shakespearean romances. The larger frame of regained unity within which the young heroes and heroines of *Star Wars* and "Allerleirauh" assume new adult roles is not encompassed by the works but contained within the modal space. Where initiation is the boundary of the action, as in "Allerleirauh," regained unity is a modal potential.

Erotic romance, moving as it does toward social integration and emphasizing the hero's public role, tends naturally to have a strong secondary plot line in low mimesis. Shakespeare's romances strongly suggest but do not quite enter the low mimetic universe in which characters are independent and autonomous entities with their own motivations and desires. As it is they relate to one another primarily as figures in a broader pattern superordinate to desire and motivation.

The remaining types of romance are less social, more introspective. They might be taken as romances of introversion. If the more extroverted romances are those of eros, these introverted romances are romances of Narcissus. Romance is roughly divided into plots that bind a movement outside the self and those that move inside.

Beowulf and *Gilgamesh* are romances of thanatos. In them the heroes are drawn to confront annihilation; in both, the earthly accomplishments shored against time feel sadly frail, even though they are the stone walls of Uruk and the great name of Beowulf.

Childhood's End, *Memories, Dreams, Reflections*, and *Siddhartha* are romances of the center, in which the heroes are driven to discover the ultimate dimension of their internal but extrapersonal identities. Self in such romances, capitalized, expresses an eternal entity unbounded by the experience of a single life.

The Lord of the Rings, *Sir Gawain and the Green Knight*, and *A Wizard of Earthsea* lead the heroes to confront a dark and morally inferior component of their identity and may be called romances of the shadow. The final binding of such romances can never be celebrative, for the hero discovers a flaw at the heart. Gollum, who began as a hobbit, acts as Frodo's

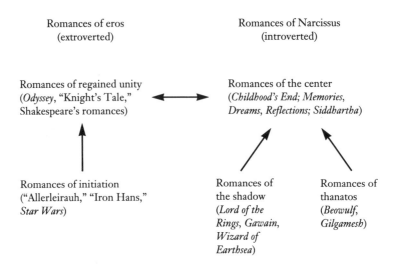

Romances of eros
(extroverted)

Romances of Narcissus
(introverted)

Romances of regained unity
(*Odyssey*, "Knight's Tale,"
Shakespeare's romances)

Romances of the center
(*Childhood's End; Memories,
Dreams, Reflections; Siddhartha*)

Romances of initiation
("Allerleirauh," "Iron Hans,"
Star Wars)

Romances of
the shadow
(*Lord of the
Rings, Gawain,
Wizard of
Earthsea*)

Romances of
thanatos
(*Beowulf,
Gilgamesh*)

FIGURE 5. Some Types of Romance

shadow. To destroy the ring it is necessary to destroy Gollum and to mutilate Frodo.

As the romance of initiation is an included subset of the romance of regained unity, and as that larger type defines the space of romances of eros, so does the romance of the center contain the other romances of Narcissus (see fig. 5). Further, the two larger types tend toward one another. When Govinda kisses Siddhartha's forehead, God becomes manifest as Samsara, the flux of phenomenal reality. At the center of self is the world. Conversely, the hieros gamos that celebrates regained unity reconciles the opposites of self and world, as in Jung's hospital visions recorded in *Memories, Dreams, Reflections*.

A larger group of works would extend the list of subgroups. For example, I am aware of an erotic romance type, the romance of epiphany, which is driven by a teleological movement toward the revelation of divinity in the extrapersonal world. Basho's *The Narrow Road to the Deep North*, *The Bhagavad Gita*, and *The Golden Ass* are romances of epiphany.

A different base set of works might have resulted in a different arrangement of subgroups. Certainly more works may be added to the list. Beyond a tidy desire to catalogue the works one knows, the purpose of developing such systems is to teach us more about a work by putting it in the company of similar works. Such a hermeneutic end might be served by alternative arrangements.

However, I make a stronger claim for the two umbrella groups, the romances of regained unity and of the center. In my current sense of romance they constitute the fundamental poles of the mode. I expect that further works would only identify further spaces within the two master types. The telos of romance is reached either by moving without or within ourselves.

The scheme of generic associations I have described works to develop meaningful parallels among deeply related works. Without some such organization we lose our way. In romance, the world cooperates and suggests order at every turn. In a universe of meaningful coincidence, the correspondences arise naturally. For example, when I devised my list of romances for this chapter, I had no notion that I would use them to develop a generic scheme. My experience in this long project generally has been to stumble on this or that seemingly at random until some general pattern in the discoveries pressed itself upon me. In romance, I must not ignore the providence with which I have cooperated in discerning an organization *that emerged in the material.*

From the point of view of the next chapter, in the universe of irony, all this is nonsense.

6

Irony and Myth

A PURELY IRONIC NARRATIVE would present a paradox of changeless-
ness and flux. Events (for without event it would not be a narrative) would
be related by sheer contingency in the ironic universe. History would collapse into an indefinite and extended present, because events could not
move continuously from one defined state to a separated future, all movement being arbitrary and directionless.

The narrative would have no medium of expression. Language would
resolve into its own arbitrary conventions for it would find no meaningful
extralinguistic relationships to express, and mimetic action would find no
principle that could distinguish its movements from whatever chaotic
spasms it imitates.

In fact, in the purely ironic universe, the nothing that observes finds
nothing to observe. Movement, being directionless, equals stasis. In its
bones, ironic narrative is antinarrative; ironic plot, antiplot.

For more than a century, we in the West have struggled against the
inherently inarticulate conditions of the ironic vision in our urgency to
express it. Antonin Artaud and Samuel Beckett convey the force of the
ironic vision. Jacques Lacan seems to be able to speak of human action
without seriously betraying irony. So speaks Jacques Derrida in literary
theory. Anyone who reads can supply additional examples. The list would
include many of the thinkers and artists who have been taken most
seriously in this century. Frye observes in the first essay of *Anatomy of
Criticism* (1969) that this is the age of irony. In theory and philosophy, at
least, the direction toward ironization has changed little since he wrote
the passage.

The challenge to ironic narration is to present an inherently inarticulate and static universe in a narrative—defined by change and developed
through verbal or visual structures, units that hang together to make a
story. Ironic narration, then, is at necessary war with its own expression.

The microstructure of any narrative at most moments tends toward low

101

mimetic reality organization. Somebody decides to do something or not to do something; a condition arises to which humans react. Only in retrospect or cumulatively, in the macrostructure of events, do we understand the true process of the plot, if indeed the plot is other than low mimetic.

The usual strategy of an ironic plot is to deny to the decisions and actions of the characters any real efficacy, as in Petronius's *Satyricon* with its central metaphor of impotence. Such a plot takes on the shape of a sine wave: things get a little better, then they get a little worse, then a little better again, and so on. (*Tristram Shandy* is fairly thoroughly ironized; Sterne could have drawn a much less complicated plot line than he does.)

In the microstructure most plot lines are discontinuous to some degree. That is, the unexpected, inexplicable, and contingent intrudes on the universe of the narrative and on the plot. Such discontinuities, when we become conscious of them, represent an ironic dimension of the plot. Victor Udwin (1987) has used the term *interruption* to describe the moment in reading when we experience a discontinuity in our consciousness of the flow of the text, the necessity of a temporary or permanent change in the way we understand what is being told.

Similarly, the psychoanalyst Barnaby B. Barratt describes in *Psychic Reality and Psychoanalytic Knowing* (1984) the rupture of semiosis that takes place when people reimagine themselves in another context. For example, we thought that the reason we had forgotten first to write, then to address, and then to stamp Aunt Susan's letter was that we were preoccupied with business matters. That understanding constitutes a semiosis, a meaning system within which we understand our action. In a moment of insight, perhaps furnished by a psychoanalytic context, we realize that we are revenging ourselves on Aunt Susan for her preference of our younger sister in our childhood. We now understand our behavior in a different way—the old semiosis has been ruptured and a new semiosis constituted. We have experienced an interruption in passing from one semiosis to another.

In Barratt's understanding, the new semiosis has no absolute epistemological value. It may be as easily ruptured as its predecessor. If values can be said to arise in Barratt's theory, they accrue to the experience of dislocation itself. In Udwin's literary term and in the aesthetics of Barratt's position, interruption becomes the point of the text. Such aesthetic values are appropriate to irony and will be familiar to most readers of twentieth-century literature and criticism. Just as critics and theorists identify interruption as a literary value within the ironic universe, so do many ironic narratives raise interruption to a fundamental plot strategy.

Besides denying the efficacy of action or employing interruption, an ironic plot such as those of the novels of Alain Robbe-Grillet may compromise the action itself, suggesting that it is indeterminate by supplying alternative descriptions or by rendering the action static through repetition. Works that incorporate randomness (for example, those that ask the reader to reshuffle the episodes for each reading, or in which the author has already shuffled them) defeat the low mimetic microstructure by denying continuity among actions; a single act of unexplained violence will have the same effect. Such antiplot devices need only be done once and cannot establish a genre because their point consists in the disruptive strategy.

Plot and Antiplot: *Waiting for Godot*

Such exhaustion of technique did not seem to have touched Samuel Beckett. He conveys an anguished need to get it said, all of it. Interruption is Beckett's most constant stylistic tool. As *Waiting for Godot* opens, Estragon is struggling to remove a boot. He battles his boots throughout the play; the boots may or may not preserve their identity, as they may or may not have been replaced by another pair between the two acts, an indeterminacy attributed to both internal and external reality in the play. The first line spoken is Estragon's "Nothing to be done." We have just seen him struggling for too long to do something ordinarily no great challenge, remove a boot. We understand the line as expressing a kind of futility usually associated with broad comedy—Laurel and Hardy managing a ladder, or Dogberry an inquiry.

Vladimir's response:

I'm beginning to come round to that opinion. All my life I've tried to put it from me, saying, Vladimir, be reasonable, you haven't yet tried everything. And I resumed the struggle. (*He broods, musing on the struggle. Turning to Estragon.*) So there you are again.

Estragon: Am I?

Vladimir leads us to interrupt our understanding of what Estragon has said, and Estragon's "Am I?" returns the favor for Vladimir's speech. The horizon of broad comedy created by "Nothing to be done" is replaced by a horizon of lugubrious reflection. Vladimir's misprision of Estragon's remark sounds intentional, the kind of willful mistake often practiced on

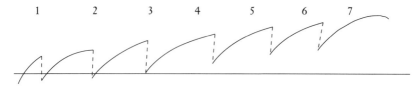

1. Estragon struggles with boots, interrupted by "Nothing to be done."
2. Vladimir reflects, interrupted by "Am I?"
3. The two friends greet, interrupted by Vladimir's admiration at the news that his friend has spent the night in a ditch. (The inappropriate valuation forces us to reunderstand the stituation—forces us to become aware of our own valuation.)
4. Discontinuous musings on suicide and friendship, interrupted by the phrase "It hurts," transferred from Estragon's boots to Vladimir's groin in a vaudevillian game of double-entendre.
5. Vladimir undertakes a fugue based on the phrase "the last moment."
6. Vladimir sets and springs a trap for the audience based on the stories of Christ and the two thieves, an interruption of the implied audience's understanding.
7. Estragon, looking over the audience, makes a mildly sarcastic comment ("Inspiring prospects") and suggests leaving. Vladimir says that they cannot because they are waiting for Godot.

FIGURE 6. Interrupted Plot Microstructure: *Waiting for Godot*

children by careless or uncaring adults, a turning of the phrase that leaves the child outside the communication. But how do we understand Estragon's "Am I?" Does he truly not know whether he is there or not? Has he undertaken some sort of misprision on his own so private that we cannot detect its horizon? Is it a serious comment on the diaphanous nature of identity, and if so an authorial intrusion in Estragon's voice? Perhaps it is best to observe that the remark constitutes for me a horizon-less interruption.

The microstructure of the opening few speeches of the play through page ten might be as represented in figure 6.

Vladimir's objection that the tramps cannot leave because they are waiting for Godot (10 verso) constitutes a plot turn in the macrostructure of the play. We now know what the two tramps are doing, the nature of the general enterprise beyond the so far disorganized and discontinuous interactions of the two characters. Entropy is by so much lessened. Of course, the plot line never moves to a final binding of this desire: Godot never appears. Instead, the plot oscillates between moments of intensity—hopefulness, disclosure, confrontation—and sloughs of confusion.

Such is the immediate microstructure of the play, establishing a verbal

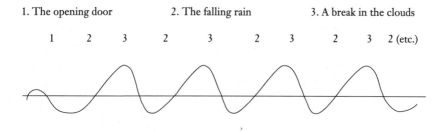

1. The opening door   2. The falling rain   3. A break in the clouds

FIGURE 7. Ironized Plot Form

texture elaborated but never abandoned. The general form of an ironic plot is represented in figure 7. Given that, as Vivian Mercier (1956) says, in *Waiting for Godot* "nothing happens, twice," and given that the plot line looks like a sine wave, how do we know (as we generally do) when we have come to the end? When an ironic plot achieves closure, as this one seems to do, it cannot be through a final binding of the plot energies.

One way to look at the ironic plot is to observe that it is driven by anxiety—fear or desire without an object. Having no object, anxiety cannot be bound. The plot can achieve a temporary binding but cannot pass on to an infernal vision. Instead it reverts to a burnt fingers stage in a potentially infinite cycle of progress and reversion. Yet Beckett's *Waiting for Godot* convinces us that we have seen the full shape of experience.

The names of the process stages in an ironized plot—the opening door, the falling rain, and a break in the clouds, leading to more rain, another break, more rain, and so forth—are meant to recall the victimization of characters by the impersonal facts of existence, and the tendency of ironized texts toward repetitions of meaningless miseries. The repeating series is the basic form of an ironized plot.

Waiting for Godot is based on cycles. Two days pass. Doubles abound—even the syllables of the main characters' nicknames, Didi and Gogo. The pitiful tree acquires a few leaves to represent the cycle of seasons. The sun plunges up and down in two diurnal cycles. (The superimposition of days and years undoes both.) Pozzo and Lucky, bound to one another in complementary futility, appear twice, as does Godot's messenger, perhaps the same boy on both appearances even though he denies it. The life cycle is represented finally by Vladimir's image of a woman giving birth astride a grave. The play is complete when we know the limits within which change occurs, and that all change will be trivial. Memory and language both struggle to discover or discount continuity, a coherence in experience. Didi tries tenaciously to get the other characters to confirm his suspicions of continuity, but they refuse. Finally it is all one whether something can be said to have happened or not, whether events and persons are unique and the result of indifferent contingencies or are part of an unvarying and static cycle, a single event. Didi reflects while Gogo struggles with his boots yet again and, defeated, goes to sleep:

> Was I sleeping, while the others suffered? Am I sleeping now? To-morrow, when I wake, or think I do, what shall I say of to-day? That with Estragon my friend, at this place, until the fall of night, I waited for Godot? That Pozzo passed, with his carrier, and that he spoke to us? Probably. But in all that what truth will there be? (58 verso)

The play performs something like an anatomy of those things that interest us about the world and ourselves, that ordinarily make life worthwhile. In that anatomy Beckett looks at them in the light of a cold eternity in which life is an accidental aberration. Sexuality becomes the erection one could look forward to having if one could manage to overcome the intricacies of getting hanged. Chicken bones and filthy roots stifle the appetite. Lucky babbles of theology and philosophy, the pleasures of the intellect, until silenced by the others who, acting for the audience, find his babbling comically intolerable. Political relationships collapse into the shifting and ambiguous roles of exploiter and exploited and of uneasy interdependence among Pozzo and Lucky, Vladimir and Estragon.

Much of the play's comedy emerges from the great energy with which the characters confront the conditions of their existence. It would be a different play if Gogo picked at his chicken bones with distaste instead of sucking on them greedily.

The audience must confront the conditions of its existence as well if it engages with the play. Didi muses that "one of the thieves was saved" (8 recto). The implied audience congratulates itself on recognizing what it takes to be a scriptural reference. A few minutes later Didi observes that of the four gospels only one (Luke) mentions the saved thief. "Of the other three two don't mention any thieves at all and the third says that both of them abused him" (9 recto). We live with verities that, on closer inspection, disappear, are interrupted. "People are bloody ignorant apes" (9 recto). That now includes us.

Synchronic Form in *Titus Andronicus*

Among Shakespeare's plays, *Titus Andronicus* has the strongest drive toward the ironic vision. While it has its share of interruptions, it uses another antiplot strategy that has received great attention in this century: an ironized version of synchronic form.

Plot (as we have used the term so far) organizes events in causal strings, analogous to syntax in language. Roman Jakobson observes that language may be imagined in two dimensions, figurally characterized by metaphor, which equates two entities, and by metonomy, which names one entity by an associated entity as in "I was just reading Shakespeare," meaning "I was just reading one of Shakespeare's plays" (1987, 95–114). Syntax, a feature of metonymic competence, relates entities as part of an ordered string, even as plot organizes functions causally.

Synchronic form in narrative is a special case of metaphoric association. So far as I understand this kind of organization, synchronic organization is as modal as is the organization by diachronic plot. *Synchronic plot* is something of a paradox, but by taking *plot* as a general term for a way in which meaning arises in a narrative experience, and by understanding that by *plot* when used alone we mean "diachronic plot," I hope that *synchronic plot* might serve as meaningful shorthand for "synchronic narrative organization."

We might expect that synchronic plots will exist in romance, high mimesis, and low mimesis, and that all three might be ironized or mythicized. Two examples are the ironized high mimetic synchronic plot of *Titus Andronicus* and the mythicized romantic synchronic plot of the trickster in American culture of the late 1960s.

Ironic strategies make the experience of *Titus Andronicus* different from that of any other Shakespearean play. Its closest Renaissance analogues are in the works of other playwrights: Christopher Marlowe's *Edward II*, Thomas Kyd's *The Spanish Tragedy*, John Webster's *The Duchess of Malfi*. Ironic strategies are strong in these plays and in other tragedies of revenge.

D. J. Palmer (1972), John Cutts (1968), Lawrence Danson (1974), Jack Reese (1970), A. C. Hamilton (1963), and Eugene Waith (1957) have all observed either directly or by implication that our emotional transaction with *Titus Andronicus* is displaced from the simple arousal of pity and terror. (Waith's 1984 Oxford Shakespeare edition provides not only a fine text but essays summarizing discussion and production of the play.) The emotional climate of the play is heavily ironized.

Our emotional involvement with any narrative is determined in part by the dynamic process of the plot and in part by the causal assumptions that allow events to connect so as to construct the plot—that is, by the play's mode. Events will derive their emotional impact partly from their relation to other events of the narrative. The same act—say, a murder—might be shocking, amusing, or neutral, depending on context.

Frye discusses the emotional tendencies of the modes in the first essay of *Anatomy of Criticism* (1969). The main plot line of *Titus Andronicus* is high mimetic, the mode of primal causation and of familial identity. Its emotional impact is cathartic—it tends first to arouse and then to allay emotion. But working counter to the cathartic tendency is irony, a mode hostile to emotional involvement.

Thomas Ravenscroft's assertion of 1678 that *Titus Andronicus* has no structure but is a "heap of rubbish" (in Waith 1984, 1) has found almost unanimous opposition lately (at least among those who have found the play worth their comments in print). Ruth Nevo (1972) has described the play's structure according to the usual plot triangle. I would like to offer an analysis of the high mimetic plot line in terms of the plot process snake.

The first stage, the violated ceremony, turns in 1.1 with the victorious general Titus's sacrifice of a son of the captured Tamora, Queen of the Goths. The scene is laid before the tomb of Titus's twenty-one slain sons. Titus proceeds to slay a twenty-second son for interfering with his wish to marry his daughter Lavinia to Saturninus, who is crowned emperor in this crowded scene.

Besides Titus's homicidal dealings with his sons and with Tamora's, the main business of the scene is to settle the succession to rule in Rome. Saturninus, baleful as his name, is contending with his brother Bassianus for the crown. It is offered to Titus, returning from triumph over the Goths, who refuses in favor of Saturninus. Denied Titus's daughter Lavinia who is betrothed to Bassianus, Saturninus takes Tamora as empress. Titus's bitter enemy because he has sacrificed her son in spite of her pleas, Tamora now shares control of Rome.

The first stage sets the problems that the play must solve. Therefore to declare its limits is to answer the question: with what does the play concern itself? The answer seems to be: with the political control of Rome and with both tender and murderous relationships among parents and children, one's own as well as those of others. Specifically, a conflict is established between Titus's family and Tamora's, and among several individual characters.

In the second stage, the fragmenting family, Saturninus, now emperor, expresses his hostility toward Titus as well as toward Saturninus's brother Bassianus. Aaron, arch-plotter of the play and Tamora's Moorish lover, sets Tamora's two sons to murder Bassianus and to rape and mutilate Lavinia and frames Titus's two sons for the murder of Bassianus. Rome becomes, in Titus's words, "a wilderness of tigers" (3.1.54) and, in the words of several characters, a bad dream.

The third stage, the climax, would ordinarily subject the energy that drives the narrative to a temporary binding. In 4.1, the sole scene of this stage, Lavinia informs her family of her abusers. On the most fundamental level of structure, Titus at this point knows and resolves to pursue the enemy. The primary complications to this simple structure are the patterns of self-mutilation and the related one of predation within the family (related because to harm one's family is to harm one's self). Titus has murdered his own son in act 1 as he urges his daughter Lavinia to suicide in act 3, scene 2, and murders her in act 5; Tamora delivers her sons to their deadliest enemy, Titus. Titus's sons more leap than fall into the blood-drinking pit in the woods, and Titus has his own hand severed on stage. Aaron tricks him into doing so, but as bloody as Aaron is, one cannot say that all the evil in the play proceeds from him or from his associate Tamora. On the level of explicit structure, the temporary binding sets into directed motion the retribution that occupies the remaining scenes of the play, but the movement is strongly countered by the impetus to self-destruction that helps lend the play its strong mood of despair.

The birth of Aaron's black son to Tamora with that event's attendant murders and its attendant division within Tamora's party is the turn of the fourth stage, the straitened course. The evil has become manifest in a parody of generational succession that promises the propagation only of evil. Titus sends messages to the impassive gods and slits the throats of Murder and Rape (actually, Tamora's two sons in allegorical disguise) brought forth from Hell by Revenge (Tamora), while Lavinia holds the barber's basin for the brothers' blood. An answering movement toward final binding is represented by Titus's brother Lucius's rallying of the Goths to his cause and against that of their recent queen, Tamora.

The final binding, the way it is, comes in two movements—a bloody imitation of the cannibalistic banquet of Thyestes, and Lucius's establishment as emperor. Titus, dressed as a cook, serves Tamora her two sons in a pasty as prelude to killing his daughter Lavinia and then Tamora. Saturninus kills Titus and is killed by Lucius. Lucius's pitilessness at the end of the play toward the dead Tamora and the doomed Aaron is a measure of the degree to which the evil announced in the beginning has not been bound, merely exhausted for the while.

Generally, the plot centers on Titus. He wrongs Tamora, is wronged by her, discovers her revenge, suffers, and takes his own revenge.

Such is the main plot line of the play. Militating against our direct involvement in its horrors are, to be sure, the aestheticizing Ovidian rhetoric of the play, but also a strong thematic pattern that runs counter to the plot line and works to render it static.

A. C. Hamilton noticed that "by the end of the first act, the tragic cycle is complete" (1963, 208). The general pattern is (1) loss of one's children, (2) violence against the children of others, and (3) murder or ingestion of one's own children. Titus has (1) lost sons. Twenty-one of his twenty-five sons have been killed; the play opens before the tomb. He (2) has Tamora's son killed as a ritual sacrifice. In trying to prevent Lavinia's abduction, he (3) kills his own son. The compressed action of the first act is repeated in broader terms throughout the remainder. Titus (1) loses two sons, (2) kills Tamora's two sons ritually, and (3) kills his own daughter. Similarly, Tamora (1) loses a son to Titus's ritual sacrifice, (2) has two of Titus's sons killed, and (3) eats her own sons in the pasty Titus has prepared. The series suggests incremental repetition, a gradual emergence of a fundamental hostility toward one's generational successors. The pattern is consistent with the high mimetic dynamics of the play.

D. J. Palmer saw that the tomb of the Andronici, the forest pit that conceals Bassianus's murdered body and into which Titus's doomed sons fall, and the terrible banquet at the end are all related in "a hideous pattern of re-enactment" (1972, 329). These three modes of entombment are related to the three movements of loss of children—to causes external to the family (the tomb), by murder of the children of others (the forest pit), and by murder of one's own children, represented by Tamora's body, which becomes the place of entombment of her own children.

The "blood-drinking" forest pit (2.3.224) with its "ragged entrails" (2.3.230) is described in strange organic metaphors that link it strongly to the banquet scene. It is called "this fell devouring receptacle, / As hateful as Cocytus' misty mouth" (2.3.235–36). Tamora is both the pit in which her two sons will be buried and the dead elder who draws them to share the pit with her. Titus promises Tamora's doomed sons that he will "bid that strumpet, your unhallowed dam, / Like to the earth swallow her own increase" (5.2.190–91).

The three modes of entombment are increasingly horrific, but each is baleful enough. The violence before all three tombs includes murders both within and outside the family. Cutting across all three is a pattern in the actions of Titus and Tamora that links each with prior and subsequent events to provide a static and geometric rather than a dynamic set of associations.

The pattern does not follow the linear experience of the plot but instead relates aggression to three great images of entombment, both by prolepsis and through retrospect, in the common manner of structural imagery. The three places of entombment are incrementally placed—they suggest one another by function and by associated imagery. Because the repetitions violate the linear movement of the plot, and because the sequential organization resolves to one act in which parents incorporate children (thereby ending generation, and their own lives, and human persistence in time), the synchronic pattern that arises acts against the plot and suggests a profoundly ironic vision of timeless annihilation. Aaron's concern for his son is a countermovement, but then all Aaron's progeny are villainies.

The effect of stasis is aided by the strong patterns of parallels in the play noticed by Hereward T. Price (1943), Palmer, and Reese. Characters, rhetorical effects, and gestures are continually used to give an effect not of progress but of repetition.

Another strongly antipathetic feature of the play is its emotional fluidity. In 1.1 Titus has been persuaded to allow his brother and sons to bury his son, whom Titus has just slain, in the family tomb. Titus, Lucius, and, finally, the ensemble engage in formal lament. Marcus then addresses his lately murderous and now grieving brother—"My lord, to step out of these dreary dumps" (1.1.391)—and proceeds to gossip about Tamora's recent promotion (indeed, within the scene) to empress, gossip in which Titus readily joins. The more somber connotation of *dumps* in the Renaissance does not rescue the passage from bathos. Yet it is in the decorum of the play, if an extreme example perhaps arising from revision. Characters typically shift emotional states in the most giddy fashion. The strategy is prominent with Titus in his mad scenes such as 3.1, something of a virtuoso piece of emotional transformation. Continuity is always embattled in this play.

Saturninus's selection in quick succession of Lavinia and then of Tamora as his empress begins the pattern of almost inexplicably rapid alternation of emotions. Tamora is brought in as a subdued enemy and presented as the triumphant consort of the emperor literally in the same scene; Titus passes from extremes of paternal devotion to absolute filicidal savagery within a few lines. The emotional energies of the play are strong but protean. Our identification with Titus as wronged hero is immediately compromised by his violence, mercurial temper, and hard heart; we are alienated in our natural empathy for all speakers by the strong and arbitrary lurches of emotional direction.

The tide of blood rises as if drawn by some cosmic gravitational pull. The characters often remark that their vision is dimmed, dazzled (e.g. 3.2.85 and 2.3.195–97), that they cannot or will not communicate (see especially 3.1.23-47, Lavinia's problem in communicating without tongue or hands, and the frustrated attempt to communicate with the gods by arrow in 4.3); action sometimes seems to lack volition. The major violator of this somnolent quality is Aaron, whose alertness seems hellish in the atmosphere of the play.

Free-floating emotional energy is anxiety. As it has no object it cannot be bound. A plot process (most simply) in which Titus is wronged and obtains his revenge is heavily undercut because the characters are not driven by emotions with objects but by anxiety. The objectlessness of the characters' hopeless anguish underlies the various thrusts toward stasis in the play, the strategies of repetition and geometric structure that arise from and convey anxiety. The plot, ironized, tends to become a repeating series of brutalizations.

In no other play by Shakespeare does anxiety lie so at the heart. Its prominence here, however, is easily matched in twentieth-century literature. The same emotional disjointedness, heavy use of devices of repetition, and atmosphere of violence and despair we find in *Titus Andronicus* we also find in Jean Genet's *The Maids*, Euguene Ionesco's *Macbett*, and Beckett's *Waiting for Godot*, not to mention popular action films. *Titus Andronicus*'s similarity to the modern theater of the absurd rests on the solid basis that it, like these ironized dramas, has anxiety at its energic core and names a contingent universe. The same may be said of other revenge tragedies but perhaps to a lesser degree; in other contemporary plays the dynamic process is more pronounced and the element of anxiety correspondingly less central than in *Titus Andronicus*.

In the company of modern ironic drama, many of *Titus Andronicus*'s traditionally remarked defects—its crudities of characterization, its repetitiveness, its constant flirtation with bathos and comedy, its violence, and its view of the futility and triviality of human life—come to seem characteristics of its modal affiliation. Surely ironic texts in general—say, Petronius's *Satyricon*, Voltaire's *Candide*, and Louis-Ferdinand Celine's *Journey to the End of Night*—share all these and other features with the play.

The high mimetic structure of *Titus Andronicus*, then, is at odds with our emotional transaction with the play. Insofar as its plot dissolves in anxiety it is not subject to final binding, to a satisfying resolution. A production of the play is likely to move in one direction or the other, toward irony or toward dynamic process.

Jacques Petit, who saw the play performed in England in 1596 on tour, wrote in a letter that the spectacle was better than the matter ("la monstre a plus valu que le sujet") (Ungerer 1961, 102). Spectacle has remained an impressive potential of the play. Twelve people were carried unconscious from one performance of the most important modern production, that of Peter Brook in 1955 (*Shakespeare Newsletter* 5.5–6, November–December 1955, 1).

The emphasis on spectacle in the production history does indicate that the static nature of the play, its tendency to tableau, has been sensed by its producers. Perhaps the fact that the post-Elizabethan stage history of *Titus Andronicus* belongs largely to the twentieth century arises from its compatibility with modern antirealistic stage traditions and audience expectations.

Titus Andronicus more readily yields an experience of the world as ironic than as high mimetic. Shakespeare seems to have stretched the received forms of the drama to their limits and beyond in pursuit of a particularly dark vision of the world. *Timon of Athens* similarly tests the limits of a low mimetic plot line.

In other plays of Shakespeare (and one could mention almost any other in illustration), anxiety motivates slight movements away from the sweep of the plot, pauses that lend complexity to our experience. I am thinking of loose ends—Jacques at the end of *As You Like It*, Don Armado at the end of *Love's Labor's Lost*, Antonio at the end of *The Merchant of Venice*, Malvolio's exit from *Twelfth Night*. I am also thinking of moments when the action pauses and the context of the action itself seems to dissolve— Macbeth hearing of his wife's suicide, or Prospero reflecting on revels' end. Sometimes, as in *King John*, *Julius Caesar*, and *Much Ado About Nothing*, the language seems infected and goes into a sort of Lacanian slide in which the characters become unsure of the relationship between signifier and signified. I take these to be some of the effects and expressions of anxiety. Yet in *Titus Andronicus* alone has Shakespeare given us a play in which plot itself is endangered by the suspicion that all our actions, perhaps, come finally to nothing.

The Counterculture Trickster:
Mythicized Synchronic Plot

Irony is different from the other three modes but paradoxically allied to myth. Irony is more the defeat of the three central narrative modes than their sibling. Irony in *Titus Andronicus* defeats a high mimetic order. Beckett's *Waiting for Godot* exhibits such heavy irony that no marked plot line emerges; it is tamed into an oscillation between the emergence of order and its defeat, usually through interruption.

Insofar as *Waiting for Godot* leaves association between Gogo and Didi, Lucky and Pozzo, as a value—however compromised by conflict, contempt, and lack of communication—the play is residually low mimetic, but the low mimetic interests here do not develop a plot line. Still, it might be said that whatever order and persistence we find in *Waiting for Godot* do not arise from irony but from the ironized. A *thoroughly* ironized text evaporates.

In the place of an evaporated irony we sometimes find a mythic presence. When Job's suffering has become most intense, when Lucius of Apuleius's *Golden Ass* has fallen to the depths of bestial misery, when Hanuman of *Journey to the West* has cooked for ages in the sealed furnace of the gods, when St. John of the Cross has entered the undoing of the dark night of the soul, when Søren Kierkegaard confronts the desert of reason, they are close to the divine presence and to personal transformation. William Burroughs and Thomas Pynchon continually suspect a universal order on the far side of irony.

The near side of irony is low mimesis—as when Lazarillo, the beggar's boy, finds happiness as the pimp to the archpriest of San Salvador in Diego Hurtado de Mendoza's *Lazarillo de Tormes* or Candide achieves Cunegonde and a garden in Voltaire's *Candide*.

Ironic narrative seems unstable, prone to transformation, because, like myth, it is an attitude toward narrative and not itself a species of narrative order. Irony, like myth, is a state of consciousness. Further, the two extremes often suggest one another.

A myth is, among other things, a story in which a culture comes to terms with the original and (simultaneously) the ultimate pattern of its existence. A widespread pattern of behavior in the counterculture of the late sixties bears an interesting relationship to mythic patterns. Some of the participants even thought of themselves as creating myth in some vague way or as living it out. Among the primary counterculture figures (one has to avoid the term *leaders*), Abbie Hoffman was the most conscious and dedicated in setting out to create "myth" with the media, but no one quite knew what the myth was about. Here is Hoffman, in a section of *Revolution for the Hell of It* entitled "Yippie!—The Media Myth": "We are living TV ads, movies. Yippie! There is no program. Program would make our movement sterile. We are living contradictions. I cannot really explain it. I do not even understand it myself" (84).

Bracketing for the moment the relationship between his activities and myth and taking his perceptions naively and literally, Hoffman, in understanding that living a contradiction was at the heart of what he was creating, was close to identifying a specific mythic tradition. I think the myth Hoffman begins to perceive is one of the most common among the mythologies of the world, that of the trickster.

Paul Radin describes the trickster as an archaic figure of wanderlust and enormous appetite—sexual, gustatory, and experiential. Kerenyi agrees that the trickster is "a single active principle" that is archaic. The trickster's component elements according to Kerenyi are "'phallic,' 'voracious,' 'sly,' 'stupid'—*the spirit of disorder, the enemy of boundaries*" (in Radin 1972, 185; Kerenyi's italics).

I would like to make one addition to the definition. Paul Radin assumed that the satirical thrust of many of the trickster episodes was not part of the primitive characters of the Winnebago tales he was editing in *The Trickster*. That is because he sees the tales as representing a developing consciousness—as recording a time when the human mind was learning the difference between profane and sacred, male and female, outside and inside. But the trickster episodes generally take place with reference to established society. A society in the primal psychic state assigned to the trickster figure by Radin, if it were possible to speak of a society at all in such a condition, would not be capable of generating such tales. The tales recording the myth of the trickster must be generated by a society to which the trickster figure is an outsider. From such a point of view, it is more natural to assume that the satirical thrust of the myth cycle is somehow an essential part of it—to notice that the trickster myth is always told with reference to an established society on which the myth cycle itself is an implicit or, from time to time, explicit comment.

Loki is a commonly mentioned trickster in Germanic mythology. "Loki's Flyting," a major poem of *The Elder Edda*, portrays Loki telling nasty satirical stories on all the other major Asgard gods. He is involved with other directly satirical incidents, as when he has Thor dressed in drag to be the bride of the ice giant Thrym. Radin's Amerindian tricksters commonly play similar tricks. They keep their societies in a continual uproar. The pose of the satirical mocker is one that I see as the trickster's customary attitude. (Jung, who takes the trickster to represent an activation of the shadow archetype, seems to make the same assumption when he centers his discussion of the trickster in Radin's book on medieval carnival traditions in which rites of the church were burlesqued.)

In this context I would locate some of the features of the counterculture in the late sixties. The counterculture was consciously archaic. Primitive life patterns were found exciting—those of the Navajos, of the dirt farmer, of the Hindu forest sage. Automobiles were as tangential to the youth culture of the late sixties as they were central to that of the fifties (although vans and cheap, dilapidated cars were okay). Technology in general became both enemy and playmate.

The counterculture was sexually active. Sexual liberation of a far earthier sort than that envisaged by *Playboy* was among its features. The goal was an absolutely casual acceptance of sex. The word *fuck* emerged into mixed company—at first hesitantly, then with glee.

The counterculture's favorite mode of relating to society was satire; it made the put-on almost a way of life. A great deal of political action amounted to satirical theater—consider the proliferation of the American flag on undershirts and toilet seats. The San Francisco Mime Troupe was one of the groups of actors that suddenly seemed at the very center of the political life of the counterculture. The phrase "guerilla theater" then current could be used to characterize a great deal of activity. Abbie Hoffman and the Yippies applied for a permit to surround the Pentagon in order to levitate it three hundred feet in the air so that it would turn orange and vibrate until all its evil emissions fled. They received the permit with the stipulation that they might levitate it only ten feet. They actually did surround the Pentagon and proceeded with the levitation ceremonies.

This type of trickster theater was carried out to ridicule the military establishment. But trickster activity did not merely constitute a subdivision of the movement against the war in Vietnam. The levitation of the

Pentagon was simultaneously a satirical attack on the morally serious and responsible mainstream of the antiwar movement.

The Yippies were as repugnant to the Students for a Democratic Society as they were to Mayor Richard Daley of Chicago; the New Left leadership was busy trying to warn people to stay away from Chicago before the police riots at the Democratic National Convention of 1968 when the Yippies nominated a pig named Pigasus for president. Ken Kesey, nonleader of the Merry Pranksters, outraged the antiwar leaders in Berkeley when he used an invitation to speak at one of the larger rallies to tell the crowd to turn their backs on the war and the antiwar and go home to work on themselves. He came to the rally in Further, the Prankster bus, which had been decorated with military slogans and supplied with fake machine guns for the trip.

Taken by themselves, the trickster activities are ironic—the undoing of connectedness, expressions of contingency, as in the "happenings" widely popular at the time. The counterculture was engaged precisely in ironizing the serious pursuits and problems of late sixties American society. The same can be said of mythic tricksters with regard to their societies.

Why did the trickster surface when it did, and what caused the figure to go away? These are presumptuous questions. They imply that we know something of the dynamics of group consciousness (beyond our intuitions). Bustling past the embarrassment of our ignorance, we may nevertheless suggest some answers. I mean the suggestions, and my arguments against them, as a discourse on the social dynamics of mythic experience.

The trickster appeared: (1) as a result of the discovery and proliferation of mind-altering drugs; (2) as a natural reaction against President Dwight Eisenhower and slushy-minded reactionary materialism (in this view, the *Reader's Digest* spawned the *Realist*); (3) because Great Men reinvented the trickster at the time (Kesey, [Paul] Krassner, [Timothy] Leary, and Hoffman might be one of the law firms advanced in such an argument); (4) because society, under great strain, regressed temporarily and the primitive figure of the trickster was reactivated by a regressive cathexis of social energy; and (5) as a conscious antiwar strategy.

The last argument envisions the Vietnam War as theater produced by top U.S. planners for a world audience to build a certain kind of public image for the country. Opponents of the war found the politics of theater and of image to be their natural medium of opposition. To attack the image of the United States by political pranks was to attack the heart of the war itself. If this argument has any validity, it provides one of the first historical vindications of the efficacy of satire.

All of these explanations offer essentially valid connections, but they all fail as causative explanations. The narratives of which they are seeds fail to represent central dimensions of the counterculture or fail in adequacy or necessity. The drugs are still here, but the ambience of the trickster is not. To say that the phenomenon under question was a natural reaction to conditions in the society at the time is empty as an explanation until one can isolate and characterize the features that caused the appearance of the trickster mentality and demonstrate that those features are sufficient to the production of the trickster. Parallels to Eisenhower, reactionary politics, and fifties materialism abound in our social history and in contemporary society, but analogies to the trickster atmosphere do not.

As for the Great Men theory, most of the great counterculture tricksters were around and active before their trickster days, and many of them are around and active now, but they were all tricksters for only one period, and that simultaneously. Moreover, the society abounded in local counterculture tricksters who were not just mimicking the famous figures but responding to the same pressures that produced the more famous names. Anyone near a college campus at the time can supply examples.

The suggestion that society temporarily regressed does not name a cause but implies an analogy between the psychic dynamics of an individual and social dynamics. This may be a valid and productive analytic framework, but it is not itself a causal explanation.

Tricksterism appeared before the Vietnam War became a major U.S. issue and disappeared before it ended; tricksterism and the antiwar movement are therefore not synonymous. Some tricksters were conscious of creating a myth, and most were sure that they were fighting against the war in some way, but they were finally as mystified by what they were doing as anyone else.

An example of how little political consciousness might be discovered at the center of activity with heavy political impact is provided by Emmet Grogan's *Ringolevio* (1972), the closest thing to a history of the San Francisco Diggers we are likely to get. *Ringolevio* is, strictly speaking, extrapolitical, in that it judges events purely by their impact on the ego of the author; the book has no perspective on social issues at all. The book's point of view is a far cry from the political consciousness of the New Left.

Perhaps, rather than looking for diachronic causes of the counterculture trickster, we might try to understand the figure in synchronic terms.

Trickster activity is ironic in that it expresses caprice or contingency, the causal modality of the ironic universe; irony in Beckett and Shakespeare has tended to static form, and synchronic analysis relates events in static form. So far as the tricksters were concerned, they were ironists. However, I will view their activities *in the context of late sixties culture* as a synchronic plot in the mode of romance. The reason is that they played a part in a teleological self-compensating social dynamic. Because this particular synchronic plot constellates the mythic archetype of the trickster, the whole complex might be called a mythicized synchronic romantic plot. The sort of meaning constructed by the counterculture trickster stands in strong contrast to the annihilating synchronic plot of *Titus Andronicus*, a truly ironic configuration.

Claude Lévi-Strauss in *Structural Anthropology* claims that the function of the trickster is to mediate a fundamental contradiction in the society (1967, 221–23). What might the counterculture trickster have mediated? Between anarchy and fascism is a movement that is based on charismatic personality cults (such as those around Ken Kesey and Abbie Hoffman) and simultaneously is without leaders. Every Yippie was empowered to define the philosophy and aims of the movement. Every person who walked into a Digger Free Store was welcome to play manager. Between the rich and the poor stand the Digger Free Stores, where you were supposed to be able to take whatever you needed free and leave what you wished as replacement, and which were actually supported almost entirely by theft, as Emmet Grogan relates in *Ringolevio*. Abbie Hoffman's *Steal This Book* is a monument to this feature of tricksterism. It is generally unavailable—library and bookstore patrons took the title seriously, as Hoffman recommended.

Between rural and urban social values is the streetwise trickster who is proud of an ability to cope with Lower East Side New York and who constantly talks about joining a rural commune and sometimes does. This was a period when people who had yet to raise a tomato became knowledgeable enthusiasts of organic gardening, and counterculture food shops in large cities tried hard to look like farmers' markets in rural Iowa. People without calluses wore Big Dad overalls.

Between black and white were the middle-class whites who, by dress and lifestyle, opted as far out of society as possible, their ideal of continual alienation being derived from their sense of black culture. "Diggers are Niggers" was the favorite Digger slogan; before the trickster phenomenon became established, Norman Mailer had voiced this self-perception with his definition of *hip* in *The White Negro*. Of course, the black community in general was as put off by the counterculture tricksters as was the white community. In fact, the counterculture was largely a white middle-class movement.

Between the general anti-intellectual America: love-it-or-leave-it public and the intellectual community that agonized over the state of the country in *The New Republic* were the educated anti-academics. When Leary dropped out it was from a research position at Harvard. Kesey and Hoffman both attended top graduate schools. The universities as centers of discourse and as the home of the leisured and politically active young are naturally sources of political action in any troubled time, but an enormous amount of hostility against the universities themselves was being expended by academics. Many students and faculty members (but not, to my knowledge, administrators) were busy trying to shut down their own schools.

Between male and female was the adoption of hair and clothing styles that made it difficult for society to tell the boys from the girls. The threat to both masculine and feminine identity gave special poignancy to attempts by society to reestablish the old sexual territories represented by such figures as John Wayne and Julie Andrews, who themselves tended to rebel (Julie Andrews, against her own public image) or to become self-caricatures (John Wayne in *The Green Berets* and elsewhere).

Between pacifism and militarism were the mean peace activists. Diggers were both streetwise predators and bearers of anarchist love for the people. The Merry Pranksters hobnobbed with the Hell's Angels, and trickster politics generally gravitated toward scenes of macho violence with troops and police.

Between technology and the spirit stood the tricksters who were enemies of the technological society and contemptuous of the discipline and knowledge that produced napalm as easily as plastic wrap. They first emerged in the underground press (which developed a wire service), manipulated the public media successfully, and, like the Merry Pranksters, found in outré uses of electronics, chemistry, and automotive technology the means for self-expression and exploration.

Between a society devoted to preserving life and a society devoted to the mass production of death were figures like Gary Snyder and Allen Ginsberg, death-conscious celebrators of life, and the Yippies, who in the most offhanded and irresponsible way went to Chicago to bring the war home by allowing the Chicago police to play U.S. soldiers while the Yippies played innocent villagers.

Between apathy and total commitment stood *Revolution for the Hell of It*.

Between the serious revolutionary New Left and the hippie drug culture stood the trickster politics of ecstasy and theater.

That list surely is not exhaustive, but I hope that it names the primary oppositions in U.S. culture during the late sixties, with the exception of the opposition between the old and the young. I do not see any clear way in which the trickster mediated this opposition, except perhaps that we seem to be dealing with a youth movement with archaic tendencies.

Consider in juxtaposition the two following quotations, one from Claude Lévi-Strauss, the other from Paul Krassner:

> Thus...the trickster is a mediator. Since his mediating function occupies a position halfway between two polar terms, he must retain something of that duality—namely an ambiguous and equivocal character. (Lévi-Strauss 1967, 223)

> Street events will be attended by theatre critics; draft resistance will become a fraternity initiation rite, guerilla warfare will be preceded by press conferences; the PTA will be investigated by HUAC; teenyboppers will burn their birth certificates in front of radio stations; tax refusers will be framed as dope pushers; black militants will be pacified with saltpeter in concentration camps; white liberals will take full page "We Protest" ads in the New York Times; armed violence will be interrupted by television commercials; the mood of neo-Christianity will be: "Fuck them, Oh Lord, they know exactly what they do!"
>
> Coincidental with the Democrats Convention there's going to be a Youth International Party—YIP—and Chicago will be invaded by a mass of *yippies*. You've just witnessed the birth of a word. No more marches. No more rallies. No more speeches. The dialogue is over, baby. Tolerance of rational dissent has become an insidious form of repression. The goal now is to disrupt an insane society.
>
> We've already applied for the permit. (Krassner, *The Realist*, August 1967 issue, published in January 1968, 20–21)

Lévi-Strauss analyzed trickster myths in such a way that the constituent units of the myth continually mediate the same basic opposition between life and death (1967, 224). I have no quarrel with his analysis, but it will not apply in this way to the counterculture trickster phenomena. I found it much more natural to range the terms of opposition randomly, for the terms do not arrange themselves neatly under two master heads. Poverty is more deathlike than lifelike, perhaps, but I do not know that poverty is more female than male (except statistically), nor that country people are more likely to be pacifists than city people. The life-death and the male-female oppositions do seem more basic than the others. If the rich-poor axis is taken as equally primary, the oppositions form a sphere. As we add axes we add dimensions; an eleven-dimensional figure would be fine with me. At any rate, the oppositions refuse to sum under two master heads as in Lévi-Strauss's examples. Of course, Lévi-Strauss *set out* to illustrate a bipolar structure for what amounted to ideological purposes.

If explanations must be dynamic—must proceed from or to causes—we are no closer now than before to knowing why the trickster appeared or disappeared. The narrative role emerged in our society without an obvious summons—except for the teleological call of the mediating state produced by the role itself. Certainly, in retrospect, the trickster makes sense in terms of the social structure of the late sixties conceived synchronically.

I have found it difficult to discover other periods in history when the trickster was as vitally important to the political and cultural life of an entire society as the figure was in the late sixties. One possible parallel is Chinese society in the third century C.E. after the dissolution of the Han dynasty when the Seven Sages of the Bamboo Grove involved great masses in trickster acts such as blocking the way of their own Chinese armies who were attempting to get through the city gates in order to protect them from invading barbarians. Some of the Seven Sages were eventually executed for such acts as urinating on a military procession and copulating with a dog in public. My failure to find more periods of central trickster activity may be due to my ignorance. Or it could be that even central tricksters have seemed to record keepers to be ephemera unworthy of preservation.

I do think that tricksterism is a mode of activity constantly open to us and that tricksters can become widely known figures without being central to society as were the tricksters of the late sixties or the Seven Sages of the Bamboo Grove. The writers and artists of the "aesthetic movement" supply many examples, as do the Dadaists. On the occasion of Duchamp's exhibition of a urinal under the title of "La Fontaine" at the Independent's Exhibition in the Grand Central Gallery, Arthur Craven attempted to deliver a lecture. Although he was too drunk to do more than curse and was frustrated in his attempt to strip, his lecture was celebrated by him and other Dadaists in later years as a major victory for Dada.

Examples of the nonfamous, noncentral trickster will probably suggest themselves to most readers on introspection. Few avoid the role entirely and forever.

Is it true, as many of the New Left felt, that the tricksters were counter-revolutionary because they trivialized politics and sapped energy that would otherwise have gone to serious political activity? I do not know, for I am not sure that the common-sense expectations about cause and effect operate in social history. I have found it better on the whole to take social events as symptomatic of a peculiar collective gestalt that is in continual process of change rather than as a link in a chain of causes and effects (in the low mimetic sense); otherwise one is often stuck with hypostatized incidentals and circular explanations. Still—if it is the duty of a Marxist to develop contradictions in the society in order to assist the revolution, the trickster as mediator of oppositions was playing a counterrevolutionary role if the Marxist metaphor applies at all to this period of social history and insofar as oppositions lead to contradictions in the Marxist sense.

Carl Kerenyi states that there are three ways for a society to dispose of tricksters (in Radin 1972, 186). Society can stress their ridiculous traits and reduce them to entertainment, as the media in this country often did with amused head shaking on news shows over Hoffman's antics or with dippy comedies such as *I Love You, Alice B. Toklas* and worse, which trivial-ized the counterculture in general.

A second way to dispose of tricksters is to make devils of them. This was Vice President Spiro Agnew's approach (before he resigned due to his own deviltry). A vigilante group of athletes on the campus of the University of Iowa, where I spent this period, selected and beat an artist so savagely that he was hospitalized for many months. They chose him only for his beard and counterculture hair style; they did not enquire about his beliefs or activities. The vigilantes shared with many people a vision of all elements of the counterculture and the antiwar movement as part of a unitary attack on the United States. Many reacted with glee to the murder of the students at Kent State. The Chicago Seven, an aftermath of the Democratic convention of 1968, would probably have been the victims of lynch mobs had they been available to the public in the proper circumstances in most towns in this country.

The third way Kerenyi suggests for a society to dispose of tricksters is to make culture heroes of them and co-opt their trickster nature. I suppose

I do think the tricksters played a heroic part in late sixties culture. Ripley Hotch, a friend who spent this period as a Berkeley graduate student, remarked to me that his primary feeling looking back on the trickster activity is "How *thin* it all was"—so few people doing such trivial things. And at the same time, how important it all seemed. I hope that I have shown that these thin acts were literally central to their place and time.

When the Hog Farm commune had to deal with a generator that refused to generate, they surrounded it and chanted to drive out the evil spirits. On the one hand, the act was pure interruption, a bottomless dislocation of continuity. (Or did they really believe that they could cure a generator by chanting? Our uncertainty that they did not so believe, our sense of their uncertainty, is part of the effect.) But once one has seen that such actions are sly and stupid at the same time, that the action mediates between technology and the spirit, it is hard to maintain the ironic vision. The action takes its place in a static pattern of romantic significance.

Because synchrony relates elements in a static pattern it cannot be characterized by causality in the ordinary sense. However, it shares with the ordinary diachronic causal patterns parallel tendencies to organize events in meaningful patterns. The synchronic plot of *Titus Andronicus* undoes generation; it represents the Earth/parents consuming the children, as if in a reversal of birth. It is a plot of annihilation and thus is ironic. Its concern with the primal patterns of the family unit marks it as high mimetic.

The counterculture tricksters participated in a synchronic plot that united all elements of the society, conjoining opposites as does the final binding of a romance.

Low mimesis relates us in our social identity. A synchronic low mimetic plot is comprised by placing people with respect to one another. The configurations of affection and distance that mark the stages of *She Stoops to Conquer*, or the "Well, here we are again" scenes of *Waiting for Godot*, or the carefully wrought social configurations of a Henry James novel, provide examples of synchrony in low mimesis.

Were the counterculture tricksters living a myth? Not in any direct sense. They were not naming absolute reality in a story experienced as eternally true and effective. But the way of being in the world named in the trickster myths found us when we perhaps most needed it. We do not always choose the narratives that order our lives. As in this case, and always to the degree that our ideas arise from causes not open to us, our stories choose us.

7

Modes, Myths, Dreams, and Narrative Experience

IN HIS DEFINITION of the modes (the first essay of *Anatomy of Criticism*), Frye expands on Aristotle's comments concerning the moral stature of the tragic hero and defines the modes by the "hero's power of action" within the world of the work (1969, 33). In Frye's system, the norms by which we judge that power are low mimetic.

The powers of all characters in all modes are our own as every narrative creates and names our experience. For that reason, and because the definition suffers from the weakness of all motif-based systems (that the same motif takes on different values in different processes), Frye's modes have been difficult to apply. Is Lear more or less powerful than we are? He begins with an act of transparent folly. He is a king, but he cannot secure even a roof for his head except through charity. Are we not looking down on a scene of bondage and frustration? Then the play must be ironic, and, indeed, Frye says that high mimetic tragedy "mingles the heroic with the ironic" (1969, 37). But Frye's definitions of high mimesis and irony are exclusive. Does Lear have "authority, passions, and powers of expression far greater than ours," as he should in high mimesis (1969, 34)? We may grant the passions and powers of expression but worry about the authority that may appear in Lear's countenance though it is ignored by the people with real power. All in all, do we have more or less power over the conditions of our existence than does Lear? One way to answer is that insofar as the play names our experience we have about the same power.

Examples would be easy to multiply. Frye's modes have seen little useful application, although their suggestive power has been appreciated for a generation now. (Hayden White's application of the modes to historiography is one interesting exception; however, because he also uses Stephen Pepper's static "root metaphor" theory, and because of the way in which I redefine the modes, I have found it impossible to dovetail my thoughts meaningfully with White's theory.)

To be fair, Frye intended to make a general historical argument with his modes, not to provide the basis for a theory of plot. It is in his theory of myths that he sketches the basis for a detailed analysis of textual structure. I have not followed his direction, the modes seeming to me the source of truer hints. Myth, as characteristic of a past stage of consciousness, has a peculiar place in our psychology and in our culture, but the other modes will not resolve to myth. In fact, the plot processes of myths are developed clearly only in the remaining modes.

Frye discerned an organization in literature. I believe that the divisions he described correspond to exclusive universes of experience, most clearly differentiated by the ways in which events are related to one another—by causal modality. The dominant types of causation (and the parallel types of synchronic association) will determine the ways in which meaning can arise. Further, freedom of action is a secondary characteristic of the narrative universes, dependent on the ways in which we can elicit or create meaning. The same can be said of our emotional relationship with a text, the second set of terms by which Frye distinguishes the modes.

Low Mimesis

From the seventeenth century until only recently (if a change has indeed occurred), low mimesis has seemed to describe the fundamental nature of reality for most guiders of our culture. The causal modality of low mimesis is proximate. Events are related through the classical cause and effect relationships: contiguity in time and space, adequacy of the cause to the effect, precedence of the cause, and the necessity of the cause to the effect. Meaning arises from human intention within the conditions imposed by causal chains. In low mimesis we are defined by our social identity: we are what we are in relation to others.

By the way, it makes no modal difference whether the characters look like rabbits, as in Richard Adams's *Watership Down*, gremlins as in the movie *Gremlins*, the living dead, body snatchers, rats, bears, wolves, or space monsters. If the main characters are busy creating order or disorder in the present through their actions, they inhabit a low mimetic universe.

Low mimetic process depends on the ability of the characters to act in accordance with their desires or fears. The mode demands that events be under human control to the extent that characters can bring about meaningful change or adapt to circumstances. To put constraints on action other than those imposed by society is to move from the center of low mimesis.

I take *She Stoops to Conquer* to represent the kind of work central to the mode. Natural constraints mean little in the play, as little as they do in Jane Austen's *Sense and Sensibility*, in *Much Ado About Nothing*, or in "Daphnis and Chloe." Survival narratives such as Stephen Crane's "The Open Boat" move toward irony as human action dwindles in efficacy in the face of natural forces. Crane's ocean still heaves through cause and effect, but the ocean is beyond human intervention. A slight further move away from the modal center in this direction is represented by William Golding's *Pincher Martin*, in which the main character's actions become an illusion. He is defeated by the ocean, which does not care for human purposes.

Ironization lies in several directions from the center. Desire itself can become implacably irrational, as are the greed and hostility of the social context in Steinbeck's *Grapes of Wrath* or Sinclair's *Jungle*. Human motivation becomes inexplicable or, as in *Candide*, blindly self-serving. The main characters become permanently and essentially isolated.

I find it helpful to think of the set of all narratives in a mode as defining a space that is potentially contiguous to other modal spaces at every point. Every new work redefines the modal space, reconfigures its boundaries. Trivial works add little new space, but great works add new territory that must be claimed by consciousness if we are to understand the necessary next thing. (To include space, in this metaphor, is to move what was only potentially understood into consciousness.)

To continue the spatial metaphor, works may employ their potential contiguity to other modes or they may not. Ironization and mythic shifts move works outside the domain of conscious narration. Ironization has this effect because it is antinarrative in its impulse. The move toward myth (say, in Nazi historical myths—see Frank Kermode's *Sense of an Ending*) leads away from conscious participation in shaping temporal change. The major present danger in this direction is the Armageddon plot that places us in the last days and welcomes the apocalypse. We will finally get ours, and *they* will get theirs.

Within the domain of conscious narration, low mimetic works may employ their proximity to high mimesis or to romance. By calling into question commonsense expectations about the organization of reality— that is, by suggesting other than proximate causal relationships among events—a low mimetic narrative can secure strong effects, whether giddy, solemn, or terrific. Tzvetan Todorov's book, *The Fantastic*, provides many examples of low mimetic works that suggest the possibility of romantic reality organization. So do South American magical realism (Gabriel Garcia Marquez's *Hundred Years of Solitude*), horror movies such as *Nightmare on Elm Street*, and many another horror movie, novel, and comic book. Books such as Leo Tolstoy's *War and Peace* and Steinbeck's *Grapes of Wrath*, which suggest a shadowy order in history, emerging within human decision but not utterly dependent on it, indicate the possibility of high mimetic realities from within low mimesis. On a lesser historical scale, Arthur Miller's *View from the Bridge* and other low mimetic works with secondary high mimetic plot lines (the film *Chinatown*, Eugene O'Neill's *Long Day's Journey Into Night*, and indeed many prestigious low mimetic narratives) employ the effect of suggesting prior organizations of experience within which the characters are trapped as they try to order their lives.

Tragedy in low mimesis arises from threats to social bonds. If in the mode we are defined by our relationships with others, the isolated person loses identity, as in Orwell's *1984*. Miller's *Death of a Salesman* with its depiction of isolation in many guises could be used to define low mimetic tragedy. Horror movies in which teenagers are knifed or consumed represent an extension in the direction of irony from those in which they suffer social isolation (*Sixteen Candles*). Tragedy and irony ought not be confused. David Lynch's *Blue Velvet* has no marked tragic dimension; like his *Eraserhead* before it and *Wild at Heart* and *Twin Peaks* after, it ironizes a clichéd low mimetic narrative universe. *Twin Peaks* kept moving toward a romantic organization, but the television series expired without making the breakthrough.

Tragedy is not so natural in the low mimetic universe as is comedy. A mode in which we imagine ourselves in our social identity, able to shape events in accordance with our intentions as they impinge on the desires and fears of others, does not in most cases move toward an imagination of the tragic failure of our efforts. Such is not the case in high mimesis.

High Mimesis

Tragedy is natural to high mimesis, a mode in which characters discover that their actions are constrained by prior patterns that determine their identity and over which they have no control. Oedipus's acquiescence, even that of Macbeth or Hamlet at the end, moves high mimesis as far toward comedy as it will go.

In an ironized narrative, tragedy and comedy are hard to separate. Beckett's *Waiting for Godot* is funnier than Celine's *Journey to the End of Night*, and William Burroughs's *Naked Lunch* is funnier than Robbe-Grillet's *Jealousy*, so some degrees of difference must be observed.

Irony is typically witty. Voltaire's *Candide* is one of the funnier books I have read. In Sterne's *Tristram Shandy*, Thomas Pynchon's *V.*, Julian Barnes's *Flaubert's Parrot*, irony provides more laughs than its student reputation indicates. Still, a distinction between the comic and the humorous is easily made. The ironic universe is neither comic nor tragic. It simply *is*, indifferent to the human contrivances by which events are lent comic or tragic dimension. The same might be said of romance, mutatis mutandis. In romance the creative and destructive potentials of the teleological dynamic manifest a unity. Comedy and tragedy in romance as in irony exist only through partial manifestations of the modal logic.

Literary works with main plot lines in high mimesis are rare but prestigious. The tragedies of Golden Age Greece and Elizabethan England furnish the only examples known to me. They all feature an emerging family dynamic. The energic drives of high mimesis are experienced as coming from both without and within, so that the high mimetic universe is charged with purpose, and external reality is drawn into the process. All Denmark is ill in *Hamlet*; Macbeth creates a hell in Scotland; Oedipus's guilt is a literal plague on Thebes; Agamemnon's murder is of universal interest, carrying out as it does a hereditary pattern of interfamilial outrage that is under the direction of the gods and expresses their interests.

In high mimetic experience, one discovers that one's identity has been determined beyond choice and beyond knowledge. A pattern emerges—in which one acts and has acted—that has been the result of choice but not of knowledgeable choice. What has seemed free or contingent has been determined by a pattern in events that one has carried about inside as a secret determinant of all that one has done.

It makes sense to me that somewhere there may be naturalistic or Marxist works in which a genetic or historical dynamic emerges in such a central way as to constitute a dominant causal modality. I have not read such works, but I can imagine them. Meanwhile, Freud among all psychologists best equips me to understand my experience of high mimetic narration, for he imagines human beings in their high mimetic definition within the family.

High mimesis, as Frye said, has a particularly strong tendency to ironization. The irresistible and indifferent course of universal process can look, in our helplessness before it, like a cosmic trap, as it does to Oedipus, Lear, and Macbeth. Job moves directly from thoroughly ironized suffering to a romantic universe in which all is organized, even if the careful God who organizes events does not observe human moral categories. *Oedipus at Colonnus* makes the same move. Perhaps because Lear's suffering is so great, some critics would like to provide the same sort of divine order or an even more moral variety for him, but I think the logic of the text will not support it. Lear looks into a void in which even the hostility and love of generations succeeding one another become contrivances, inspiring games such as Edgar's project of judicial combat to produce justice and order, or such as the drama whereby Gloucester is saved from a painted devil by a shammed divine intervention. Supporting all our contrivances of love, hate, and justice is exactly nothing. The universe is such that a wholly innocent Cordelia can die through sheer accident, causelessly and needlessly, after Edmund's deathbed decision to remedy his command to have her killed, acquiescing to Edgar's moral plot for events. Universal process is no more interested in his moral drama than in any other. Although the main plot line of *Lear* is high mimetic, it ends by suggesting a world of sheer contingency, a glimpse of the ironic vision.

Macbeth, on the other hand, ends by suggesting a romantic order in which all accidents were meaningful and pointed toward a future state (the orderly succession of English rulers and the state's permanent glory). In high mimetic space, *Lear* is contiguous to *Titus Andronicus* and *Macbeth* to a romance such as *Cymbeline*, another play with a romantic imperial vision.

Yet *Macbeth* is not a romance. Macbeth follows the iron course of intergenerational predation to its termination. In killing his king-father, he has ensured sterility for himself. The son who murders the father to become the father has committed violence against himself. (Duncan acts as a father in that he is the source of Macbeth's legacy, his power and place in society; generational succession is of course a major metaphor in the play.)

In low mimesis, characters construct a meaningful order in the present. In high mimesis, characters discover an order that has always shaped events but that they have not before discerned. In romance, characters construct a future state in harmony with a general movement in the world at large.

Romance

The scope of orderly change—the breadth of the effect that characters have upon their world—generally increases as one moves from irony to low mimesis to high mimesis to romance, as Frye indicated in his discussion of freedom of action. In ironized narratives, the characters have little effect on their worlds. In low mimetic narratives, the characters' actions tend to resonate in their immediate society. That generalization must admit many exceptions and identifies only a modal tendency, arising from causal modality. In most low mimetic works we do not imagine human beings as able to influence broad-scale events through their actions. In those works that have main plot lines in low mimesis but treat whole societies, such as Tolstoy's *War and Peace* and Orwell's *1984*, whatever universal processes are suggested do not belong to the main plot line. In low mimetic science fiction, such as Larry Niven's *Ringworld*, characters are able to create worlds and alter solar systems, but by modal demand they follow no universal plan in doing so. We are most free in low mimesis.

In high mimesis we are most constrained. Oedipus's struggle against the terrible order of his life provides the model of the problem, and his acquiescence, the model of resolution. Yet the scope of Oedipus's narrative reaches beyond the human world, beyond that over which we might have control. In the typical romance, the scope is cosmic. On the actions of Frodo Baggins and Sir Gawain depend the fabric of their realities. (Gawain's fault is a fall from golden perfection into the Green World of flawed nature, and all knights wear the sign of the fall after Gawain has slipped.)

In romance it is as if the limits of our being became universal, as if we expressed some universal becoming. Fritjof Capra's *The Tao of Physics* thus expresses a world view consistent with romantic causal modality. Romantic thinking is still considered "soft" by the intellectual community at large, East and West. Yet the denial of romance has nothing more to recommend it than a modal value judgement.

In Vonnegut's ironized romance *The Sirens of Titan*, the universal process of becoming is absolutely trivial. Human history has labored to produce a spare part for a space ship so that a robot can deliver a message to the farthest part of the universe: a single dot, signifying "Greetings." The romances of thanatos by virtue of their concern with annihilation move toward irony. As with all narrative, ironization may be suggested at any point through any of the techniques of contingency and stasis.

Romances of initiation commonly suggest their contiguity to low and high mimesis. As main characters move into their appropriate social identities they confront the problems of family and society that are the stuff of those two modes. Thus *The Odyssey* will yield a secondary plot line in low mimesis that emphasizes the restoration of a just order on Ithaca and a high mimetic plot line emphasizing the relationship of Telemachus and Odysseus.

Narcissistic romances less commonly employ low or high mimetic organizations. Concerned as they are with internal states, these romances do not often attribute the degree of autonomy and importance to personalities necessary to generate low and high mimetic plot lines. Yet in any social interaction, low mimetic modality momentarily suggests itself and, in any serious consideration of family, high mimetic.

Myth and Irony

I only wish to emphasize here that myth and irony have special status among the modes, and a special relationship to one another. They are things that can happen to narratives. Myth raises narrative to a universal principle of organization. Irony reveals a void on which we construct all our narratives. Irony moves toward stasis, a vision of a universe without significant change and therefore without meaning. But myth also moves toward a vision of the universe as one perfect whole, changeless and perfectly significant. The plenum and the void are two contraries that constantly suggest one another. This ancient truth lies at the point where narrative disappears.

Dream, Myth, and the Nature of Narrative

The telling of stories is both universal and difficult to explain. Why should we spend so much time telling one another tales? For pleasure, says an Aristotelian voice. But to observe that stories entertain us is to say that stories interest us—that we value them. Why?

An activity as universal and as insistent as the sharing of tales must serve some function in our lives. Do all stories serve some general purpose that underlies our pleasure in them? Or no general purpose at all but as many purposes as stories? Or fewer, so that one class of stories serves purposes that others do not?

If stories had no relationship at all to our experiences before and after the stories, they would be strictly inexplicable. But most stories do not imagine such ironic depth and none achieve it.

Aristotle observed in his *Poetics* that we delight in mimesis, "imitation" in a sense broad enough to include dance as a way of imitating and impossibilities among the imitations. J. R. R. Tolkien called that which we create through imagination by art a "sub-creation" (47). The reality of a story is secondary, as he says: secondary to whatever is prior to imaginative experience, including silence. We imitate the world; the world that we imitate is only our experience of the world, since we do not apprehend it directly but through the creative process of perception. In tales, then, we imitate our experience of the world in an act of subcreation. A story is a naming of experience. Mime reminds us that language is not essential to a story; this naming may be silent. In any case, that with which we do the naming is largely supplied by familiar tradition. That which is named is novel. The act of naming is central to our creative engagement with the world.

Renee Fuller in "The Story as Engram: Is It Fundamental To Thinking?" (1982) reports that some profoundly retarded people understand written language only when it tells a story. Some people she has observed, not necessarily the most retarded, are incapable of understanding stories. (Most children of two are already able to do so.) She finds that when we cannot understand stories, neither can we understand who or where we are.

Certainly some stories have been important to our general identity. The Book of Revelation provides a universal plot within which many people in our culture still locate themselves. The Christian plot itself arises in the context of the general story of Yahweh's selection of Israel for glory, suffering, and justification. Traditional Marxist history is almost as thoroughly plotted and awaits a vaguely similar millennium. Stories, then, can embody a national or cultural destiny. More generally, they can give a shape to our existence in time. In fact, when we make sense of history it is sometimes by seeing in events a story.

The modern suspicion that the story is ours and not history's may be a useful assumption as we try to understand why, say, Livy chose to describe the early kings of Rome in the way he did, closer to mythological than to historical figures. Distrust of the narrative element of history implies that when one writes history one should try to avoid making a narrative of one's work. However, the story is hard to remove from history.

Mark Phillips in "The Revival of Narrative: Thoughts on a Current Historiographical Debate" (1983–84) describes the difficulty historians have had in deciding what is and is not narrative as they move back to writing it. Gertrude Himmelfarb (1984) maintains that in trying to avoid writing narrative history, historians have impoverished their work, imparting to it an ideological inclination to the minutiae of material existence while missing broad patterns of change. Determinedly non-narrative history may even fail to register the impact of significant events such as the American Revolution that are emergent in the general life of a community and that may not be linked to specifiable material conditions in the life of the part of that community under consideration. Himmelfarb takes the position that in writing history we both discern and create order and cannot do one without the other.

When we elicit a narrative from historical material, we necessarily engage in shaping the past. An analogous involvement of the observer in the event obtains in quantum mechanics. What is more, the logic of that theory suggests the possibility of reversing the usual temporal order of cause and effect. According to "Backward Glance," a *Scientific American* article in April 1985, an observation on Thursday might be said in some sense to have caused an observation of the preceding Tuesday. A generally similar situation arises when we shape the past, insofar as the past exists in our conception of it. Our shaping imagination reorders the past. Does the past itself lead us to imagine it in the way we do? Are we absolutely free to do with it what we will? Or can we identify the degrees of freedom—the constraints on, the channels of our will? I hope that modal theory indicates some of our degrees of freedom and of direction.

The order that may be in history fascinates us. Thomas Pynchon's novels turn on the possibility that we are caught in an unfolding half-glimpsed story, one that does not seem in Pynchon's conception to have the good of the human race at heart. D. H. Thomas's *White Hotel* moves from fictionalized biography (including a real Freud) to a passage that quotes an eyewitness account of the Nazi massacre of Jews at Babi Yar and ends in a revisionist heaven imagined as post–World War II Palestine under benevolent British management. At least in literature, possible patterns in historical experience continue to emerge in our consciousness.

Fiction need not have an explicit historiographical dimension to be concerned with our location in time. Frank Kermode in *The Sense of an Ending* does a fine job of conveying the drive we have for plottedness, and of tracing the insistence of a particular temporal location in our cultural tradition. Kermode sees temporal location—plottedness—as a deep need, but also as dangerous. He means to warn us that when we forget the fictive nature of the plots we spin, we are at their mercy, as Germany was at the mercy of the mythology of the Third Reich (1967, 38–41). Kermode warns us that we are now in danger of enacting an Armageddon plot.

To agree fully that all narrative arises from an ordering activity of the mind, as Kermode seriously asks, is to withdraw from the possibility of a meaning beyond artifice. Kermode has moved farther in this direction since 1967, as have most of our best literary theorists. But the pattern of every full life is inherent in the human condition: birth, puberty, maturity, senescence, death. The cycle of the seasons would continue without a percipient human to find that order. Larger patterns, such as those of evolutionary development, provide models of emergent plottedness in the history of life on Earth. Our sense of evolutionary order depends indeed on our ordering imagination. But to some extent, this side of sterile solipsism, an order arises in the data themselves. In fact, all organizations of energy in the universe, on whatever scale, from the photon to superclusters of galaxies, pass from nonbeing to being and again to nonbeing, and often do so in intricately patterned ways.

William Blake's Proverb of Hell, "Every thing possible to be believ'd is an image of truth" (1953, 126), can serve as a central principle for the strenuous imagination alone but admonishes us all to a necessary openness to the world. It *is* a proverb of hell and therefore summons its contrary. The epigraph from Nietzsche that Kermode uses for his chapter "Fictions" in *The Sense of an Ending* could serve: "What can be thought must certainly be a fiction" (1967, 34).

The story finds us as we tell it. Narrative is everywhere and has for as long as we know been one of the major ways we and the world—together—make sense. In the reach of time available to us, the status and manner of narration have changed, and so, therefore, has our sense of reality.

A continuous narrative tradition in the West reaches back to the earliest records. *Gilgamesh* has as good a claim as any to be the story of most venerable record. By the time fragments of the story were first inscribed on clay (four thousand years ago), close to the dawn of writing, the Sumerians were already masters of narration.

In the earliest stages of culture available to us stories hold a central importance. In myth people name the fundamental nature of reality in a story. No other kinds of stories seem quite so important to the people who tell them.

But myths are still not the first stories. Before myth, before language, perhaps, comes the dream. Since dreams are sometimes stories, and ones we cannot help telling ourselves, perhaps a general purpose or set of purposes for stories should be sought there.

Dreams are a part of our distant past and of the mundane and universal present. Everyone dreams every night. Infants dream in the womb (of what?), so far as we can tell from the physiological evidence. Most mammals give every indication of dreaming, save for the anomalous spiny anteater. (Benjamin Wolman's *Handbook of Dreams* [1979] is a handy and authoritative summary of modern dream research to 1979; much of what I will say about dreams is drawn from it, from Robert Haskell's 1986 special edition of *The Journal of Mind and Behavior* entitled *Cognition and Dream Research*, and from Harry Hunt's 1989 study *The Multiplicity of Dreams*, which stands almost alone in its awareness of both the sleep lab and the psychoanalytic tradition.)

Discussion of the status of the dream is suffused with doubt. As early as Plato's *Theatetus* (158.a–d) popular culture was transmitting the proposition that no one could prove that they were not dreaming at any given time; Socrates refers to the opinion as common. A famous statement of this skeptical proposition, written in the century following Socrates', is Chuang Tzu's Taoist parable of the butterfly.

> Once upon a time, Chuang Chou <i.e., Chuang Tzu> dreamed that he was a butterfly, a butterfly fluttering about, enjoying itself. It did not know that it was Chuang Chou. Suddenly he awoke with a start and he was Chuang Chou again. But he did not know whether he was Chuang Chou who had dreamed that he was a butterfly, or whether he was a butterfly dreaming that he was Chuang Chou. Between Chuang Chou and the butterfly there must be some distinction. This is what is called the transformation of things. (Bary, Chan, and Watson 1960, 73)

Do we not create all those stories we tell ourselves every night? Are we not playing all the characters, speaking all their lines in some part of our self? The transformation of which Chuang Tzu speaks is real. The dialogic imagination is fundamental to dream.

We do usually sense some continuity between what we are in our dreams and what we are waking. The continuity, however, is subtle. To dream that one is a butterfly has an air of literary artifice, but it need not be one: an acquaintance of mine dreamed he was a bird, which is not so far from a butterfly. In whatever form we assume, we manage to see the dream from the point of view of a dream ego who watches the flow of parts of the self we experience as other. Chuang Tzu implies that in the relation between the dreaming consciousness on the one hand and the dream it produces on the other lies a model of identity.

Except under extraordinary conditions we are not able to reflect on our state of dreaming until after the fact. The major exception is the unusual but not exotic type of dream called lucid, in which we seem to wake to consciousness while dreaming. (Charles Tart has an excellent chapter in Wolman's *Handbook of Dreams* [1979] on lucid dreams.) But ordinarily the dream is primary in our awareness while it occurs.

In the tradition of British empiricism, within which much of academic psychology has developed, identity is an epiphenomenon that rises to the top of experience like a froth. We are simply what the world makes of us. In this tradition, consciousness, as I recall B.F. Skinner having said in some lost context, is an unnecessary hypothesis. Such an agnosticism with regard to consciousness might lead one to whittle the dream ego out of the dream altogether. Norman Malcolm's *Dreaming* (1959) accomplishes this.

Malcolm maintains that since we cannot by definition be conscious of being asleep and must be asleep to dream, we cannot be aware of a dream per se but only of its report (1959, 66, 109). We must equate the dream to the dream report. The only behavior we can observe directly is a person reporting something that the person dreamed. The report, for Malcolm, is the dream. The position turns traditional dream skepticism on its head. "Don't worry about proving that you are not now dreaming. Prove to me that you ever dreamed." Since we can hear the screams of someone in the grip of a nightmare, Malcolm concludes that nightmares must be a special case—of screaming, for the person is not in the condition that we usually intend to express when we say "He is asleep" (1959, 62–63).

In experiments performed since Malcolm wrote his book people have been observed dreaming dreams other than nightmares. These subjects have succeeded in signaling to observers by finger twitches and eye movements that they are dreaming and have conveyed something of the content of the dream through a prearranged code. Through posthypnotic suggestion people have been induced to describe their dream verbally, while asleep (although not asleep, admittedly, by Malcolm's criteria) and presumably while dreaming (Wolman 1979, 44; Haskell 1986, 164).

As direct in its own fashion was an experiment performed on a cat. That portion of the cat's brain that inhibits muscular movement in sleep was removed. The cat, from time to time while asleep, would perform such acts as running. Brain wave activity, analogous to similar patterns in dreaming humans, indicated that the cat was dreaming, perhaps about running (Wolman 1979, 104). Malcolm's position with regard to all such observations is that no matter what we can observe, it yet does not add up exactly to a dream.

Without brain surgery I often observe myself dreaming. That is, I see no reasons other than dispensable ideological ones to ignore my experience as a dream ego. The lucid dream, in which we are fully conscious and yet dreaming and aware of doing so, is the most persuasive experiential refutation of Malcolm's position. But to refute him on his terms, I would have to show him my dream. Technology has not yet taken us so far, although such science fiction stories as Le Guin's "The Lathe of Heaven" have. (Dunlop's 1977 collection of articles, *Philosophical Essays on Dreaming*, contains several reactions by philosophers to Malcolm's position.)

Meanwhile, even some nonmammals such as birds show states that may be homologous with the REM (from the rapid eye movements of this stage of sleep) State associated with dreaming in mammals (Snyder 1966, 126). Perhaps snails dream, and we do not know the signs.

Content analysis shows that different types of persons have different types of dreams, and that age, sex, culture, and life situation all have their impact on our dreams. (Carolyn Winget and Milton Kramer provide a summary of content analyses to 1979 in their *Dimensions of Dreams*, published that year.)

Anything so common as dreaming is probably important to the dreamer. And dreams, at least human dreams, are often cast in narrative form. While some dreams are single images or single words, most tell a story. In fact, the storylike quality of REM dreams is often remarked as a distinction between them and the stream of thought we experience in non-REM sleep, the so-called NREM dreams.

All our stories surely find their primitive model in those stories we tell ourselves every night, those we have been telling ourselves for millions of years. Our confusions about the reality relationships of dreams, about their purpose (if any) and meaning (if any), find counterparts in our confusions about stories.

If we knew more about dreams we would know more about stories in general. What are the functions of dreams, if they have any functions at all? In what fashion are they produced? What do they have to do with waking reality? How do they relate to the personality of the dreamer, and to the dreams of others?

Freud was right in postdating his *Interpretation of Dreams* from 1899 to 1900; it is the first work of this century, as he said. Freud's works and those of his followers and apostates have much to tell us about dreams. The second great tradition of dream research is that of the sleep laboratories that were founded by academic psychologists following the research on brain waves and rapid eye movement in the 1950s.

Harry Hunt observes that dreams need have no more single purpose than such other basic activities as walking. Harry Fiss's caution is worth posting at the door of the discussion that follows: "One thing we can be pretty sure of: dreams probably have not a function but multiple functions" (1979, 63). Notice the qualifiers in Fiss's statement: *pretty*, *probably*. They are not empty dodges. Ninety years of psychoanalysis and four decades of sleep laboratory research have produced no consensus on dreams. Yet we know some interesting things.

The null hypothesis, that dreams are meaningless, a random discharge of energy, is counterindicated as a general principle by every successful dream interpretation. Too, the null hypothesis can be maintained only with great difficulty against positive results from REM State deprivation experiments. After deprivation, REM sleep increases temporarily in a rebound effect. Also, REM deprivation causes subtle behavioral changes. The need itself is urgent enough. Cats deprived of REM sleep for thirty days rebound with a vengeance: "the muscular twitches and eye movements become so frantic [when they are again allowed REM sleep] as to resemble myoclonic convulsions" (Snyder 1966, 124). Persons deprived of REM sleep show an increase in such drive-related behavior as sexual activity, hunger, and aggression. They act immaturely. They also are less well adapted to change in their lives. (Harry Fiss's article in the special issue of the *Journal of Mind and Behavior* [Haskell 1986] goes into interesting detail on the effects of both dream deprivation and dream enhancement.) It is no longer possible to argue that dreams serve no function at all because their absence has such effects.

It is, however, possible to argue that dreams serve only physiological purposes and are essentially meaningless when considered as ruminations on experience. The most widely publicized statement of this modern form of the null hypothesis is the 1983 *Nature* article by Francis Crick and Graeme Mitchison holding that REM sleep is a necessary discharge of excess excitation generated as the brain in its waking state engaged the world. To recall and pay attention to dreams is to stand a chance of defeating that cathartic purpose. The authors recall a split-brain experiment in which the left brain was surgically severed from its fellow hemisphere. The left brain contains the speech centers. When one's corpus callosum is severed, one's left hand literally does not know why one's right hand is doing whatever it does, nor does the left eye know what the right eye sees. But the left brain will smoothly concoct reasons for the behavior it observes being guided by the alienated right brain. Given the powerful capacity of the verbal imagination to construct meaning and connection even where none exists, Crick and Mitchison find no reason to credit the psychoanalytic tradition or any tradition that finds sense in dream content (Haskell 1986, 239–40).

But Crick and Mitchison's argument applies no more specifically to dream analysis than to analysis of any human endeavor. While the experiment does say something interesting about the creative nature of our engagement with reality, a person suffering split brain functions is under pressure to maintain psychological integrity and cannot be used as an example of normal human rationality. The relevance of dream content to human experience is so universally and manifoldly demonstrated that the authors' position itself becomes a puzzle, as does the interest it has aroused. (See Montague Ullman and Edward Storm's "Dreaming and the Dream: Social and Personal Perspectives" [Haskell 1986] for an extended analysis of Crick and Mitchison's position. They note that the meaning of a dream is personal, not public and quantitative.)

Based on observations of the properties of simple interactive systems, the Crick and Mitchison position covertly expresses a preference for seeing human beings in a certain way—as soft cyborgs, one might say, in a universe of random events. The null hypothesis is a description in the ironic mode of dreams. In modes more tolerant of significance, dreams are imagined as more significant. But within a universe defined so as to bring into doubt the emergence of any meaning (as opposed to function), the position becomes compelling. Many people in our culture share, gleefully or grudgingly, the sense that the universe is indeed like that at bottom.

As Ullman and Storm say in their article collected by Haskell, one counterindication of the Crick and Mitchison position is that our greatest interest in a dream does not come at the beginning. One would suppose that if the purpose of the dream were to discharge a certain quantity of excess energy, the urgency of our involvement would dwindle as the energy drained away into the dream. But people need to complete their dreams even more than they need to dream. The rebound effect—that is, the increased time devoted to dreaming after dream deprivation—is greater for people whose dreams are interrupted than it is for those whose dreams are prevented altogether (Wolman 1979, 55). We demand more urgently that a story be completed than that it be told in the first place.

I will not recite purposes that have been proposed for the dream. Instead, I will describe an idea that is consistent with most nonironic theoretical discussion, and that has rich implications for narrative theory: that dreams serve to integrate new experiences with those of the past. Stanley Palombo in the *American Journal of Psychiatry* reports that forty-six of fifty consecutive dreams among his patients were associated by them with "early events whose images appeared in the dream" (1984, 1508). Psychotherapy is based on the proposition that those images of early events serve, at least in part, to refer to the most significant events of our lives, those which are the basis of what Norman Holland calls our identity theme (1985, chap. 8, "The Birth of an I").

David Cohen in chapter 10 of *Sleep and Dreaming: Origins, Nature & Functions* (1979) summarizes well the research on a more general form of Palombo's claim, first advanced in 1942, that dreams are determinants of adaptation to life conditions. Most of the sleep lab research on the question has studied the effects of REM State deprivation. Cohen rightly urges that in addition we study dream content to see whether an adaptation to identifiable changes in the dreamer's life emerges; he provides some examples. Articles by Robert Smith, Rosalind Cartwright, and Stanley Krippner collected by Haskell (1986) indicate different directions now being pursued as people investigate the adaptive function of dreams. Use of dreams for both diagnosis and therapy is of course central to the psychoanalytic tradition.

Numerous types of dream-effected adaptation to life situations have been proposed by theorists. Functions include "environmental mastery, conflict and problem solving, information storage and processing, mood regulation, self-awareness, self-esteem, and ego-integration or consolidation. Some contemporary theorists have also approached the contribution of dreams to creativity" (Wolman 1979, 66).

Palombo's form of the adaptation claim is particularly interesting because it focuses on the role of the dream in determining historical identity. In the dream, what we are is adjusted by being brought into juxtaposition with what we are becoming; that is, with the changing conditions of our existence. Through dreams we adapt to the world as we experience it afresh, adjusting our historical self, and therefore our sense of identity, to allow for what surprises us. The new is assimilated by being associated with the familiar; the familiar is adjusted by being associated with the new.

John Dewey said in 1934 that art as made and as perceived remakes "past experiences so that they can enter integrally into a new pattern" (1976, 138). Indeed, as he says, "the conscious adjustment of the new and the old is imagination" (1976, 272).

Marshall W. Alcorn, Jr., and Mark Bracher advance in *PMLA* an idea suggested by the title of their article: "Literature, Psychoanalysis, and the Re-Formation of the Self: A New Direction for Reader-Response Theory" (1985). Palombo has found that in dreams we adjust our sense of the past, and therefore of our identity. The common element between his ideas and those expressed in the Alcorn and Bracher article lies in the role of the imagination as it creates and sustains identity. Alcorn and Bracher draw an analogy between the experience of fiction and the creative exploration of self in the transference neurosis, in which the patient treats the analyst as if the analyst were a significant figure from the patient's past. The transference, narrative literature, and dreams share this feature: they are all imaginative subcreations expressive of one's sense of the coherence of experience. All engage us in the imaginative reconstruction of our own identity. Peter Brooks in chapter 8 of *Reading for the Plot* (1984) discusses transference as a model for the transaction between teller and listener. The soul is the part that watches the dream; yet the dream takes on the coloration of the watching soul and helps, in its turn, determine the nature of the soul past the end of the story.

I have emphasized change here. But dreams and stories also assert the continuity of identity that underlies all the variations of a life. In chapter 3 of *The I* (1985), Holland shows through case histories how neither psychoanalysis nor the most extreme techniques of brainwashing (by the Chinese captors of a French medical doctor over a period of several years) succeeded in altering essential identity. I see no destructive contradiction between the approach of Holland and that of Alcorn and Bracher. "Without Contraries is no progression" (Blake 1953, 123). Dreams and stories name what we are and name that *what* in a novel context that, by its nature as an expression of identity, constitutes a partial redefinition of that identity. We need no experiments to confirm this proposition so long as we do not disown our expressions of identity, which constitute the field within which identity themes can arise and become available to analysis.

In stories, while awake and with far greater conscious control, we do the same sort of thing that we do beyond our volition every night. We name experience. The question now becomes not what connection dreams have to stories, but what stories do that dreams cannot. After all, if our needs were satisfied by our dreams we would not need stories, much less psychoanalysis.

Obviously, distinctions must be maintained. Perhaps one significant distinction lies in the conscious dimension of stories. John Dewey's observation that purpose, a willed ordering, distinguishes esthetic narrative from dream and reverie rests on a distinction between conscious and unconscious order but undervalues the tacit dimension of meaning (1976, 276). As Brooks says, all stories claim "to retrace event in order to make it available to consciousness" (1984, 34). They allow us to bring to conscious scrutiny representations of order and disorder that we cannot yet (or just cannot) make entirely explicit. For if the dimension of order were capable of being represented directly, perhaps we would not need to cast it in the form of a story. From this point of view a narrative is a necessary indirection.

Generally, then, both the psychoanalytic and (to a lesser extent) dream laboratory traditions view the dream as responding to the unassimilated present (and, perhaps, the future) in terms of the past. Beyond this most general assertion disputes arise. Freud emphasizes the way in which powerfully charged moments from the personal past intrude themselves in the guise of those indifferent moments of the present that provide the stuff of which the dream is constructed (that is, the past two days of the dreamer's experience); Jung emphasizes the role of the extrapersonal past in adapting to a future of which the dreamer is not yet aware. The sleep laboratory tradition has been less interested in past or future but has much to say about the dream in the present. I would like to elaborate on the modal organization among dream theories to suggest a set of observations on narrative generally.

Freud speaks as if dreams reveal a preexistent order. What we experience of a dream is only the surface, a manifest content that arises from the latent content. Latent content itself arises from our distant personal past as received by the primordial structures of our psyche. That is, Freud takes a high mimetic approach to the dream.

Harry Fiss views dreams as adaptations to a social situation in the present, a low mimetic approach. He is interested in the implications of Heinz Kohut's self psychology for the understanding of dreams. Most ego psychologists would find his view of dreams consistent with their own, as would most sleep lab psychologists interested in questions of meaning as well as of physiology.

C. G. Jung speaks of dreams as goal-directed—as adapting the dreamer to change toward some point in the future, in the familiar romantic dynamic.

Crick and Mitchison speak of dreams so as to undo ironically the artifices of meaning they find there.

The four approaches are based on conflicting conceptions of the fundamental connectedness of experience. The causal modalities of their world conceptions contradict one another.

For Freud, meaning originates in the latent content, arising from a primal past. For Fiss, meaning arises in the social present. For Jung, meaning flows into the present from the future. For Crick and Mitchison, meaning (though not function) is baseless. We must not expect these theorists to make much sense of one another. Yet on their own terms, within their own universes, they all make very good sense. If we find one making better sense than another, we may derive from that value judgment the knowledge that we prefer one universe over another.

The kind of universe we live in may not be entirely under our conscious control. If dreams—and stories—furnish a context for our sense of identity, we usually think of them as *our* dreams and stories, at least. But this habitual sense of possession has slim support.

The research on telepathy in dreams by Montague Ullman and others demonstrates that we can and do dream shared dreams (see Ullman, Krippner, and Vaughan, *Dream Telepathy*, 1973). *To invent* is (in the word's Latin derivation) to come upon, to find. Stories and dreams are public in a peculiar way. We come upon them in a space shared at least sometimes by others.

In my readings on dreams I do not find people much concerned with distinctions between fiction and nonfiction. Dreams are obviously fictive (in our culture), and they obviously, to most theorists, concern waking experience—they are fictions of experience. A similar attitude toward narrative literature would spare it trivialization.

Most of the observations I have reported concerning dreams reverberate in narrative as a whole. Dreams are partially shared, partially personal namings of novel experience in familiar terms that serve, among other purposes, to provide us with a coherent and continuous identity in space and time, except when experienced ironically. The watcher of the dream is a model of the subject. A primary distinction between a dream and waking narration lies in the dimension of conscious control, although waking and sleeping cognition may be distinguished in other significant ways. Dreams may be understood as occurring in at least four universes of signification, distinguished by the dominant causal modality. Dreams suggest that narration constitutes a fundamental activity of the mind as it engages experience.

The earliest waking stories may be myths, which are the most public, the most deeply shared, of all narratives. "Individual myth" is a self-contradictory expression.

I see no need for a stage intermediate between dream and myth. I believe that in recalling the way I apprehended certain stories, rituals, and perceptions in my childhood I am closest to understanding the experience of myth. I am still not sure whether at the age of about seven I dreamed the treasure scattered among carrot scrapings in the kitchen sink or mistook the contents of the sink while I was awake. The memory has the quality of a waking dream. Myth seems to have just this quality when it is alive and not a sentimental reconstruction.

By sentimental reconstruction I mean a retelling of the stories by someone who, like Ovid, no longer depends on them for his sense of fundamental reality. Mircea Eliade observes that the most familiar mythologies—Greek, Egyptian, and Hindu, for example—have already lost their primitive character by the time they are recorded (1963, 4–5). I will refer to these stories in the usual way as myths, but by mythic consciousness I mean not the frame of mind of Homer or Hesiod but of their silent predecessors who lived inside their myths.

Myths lose their central place in a culture, and therefore become less than myth, when a culture develops a sense of its peculiar, mundane history and contacts other cultures that it knows to be different. In that fall from innocence its stories become contingent, provisionally true to fit a changing reality. A myth can only express our relationship to a reality that follows an ordained pattern. By its nature a myth is always true. To be perceived as a myth it must be thought to exist outside of the human imagination and to be beyond change (although different versions may be freely entertained by the same individual).

Do our dreams change as we move from the mythic stage of narration? It may be some evidence that the dreams of Gilgamesh and Enkidu, and of Jacob, and of Nebuchadnezzar are revelations from the realm of absolute truth. John F. Priest remarks that dreams, divination, and the word of God are all equivalent as disclosures of the divine will in the Old Testament (1970, 64–65). The same may be said of dreams as conceived in some Oriental sources—for example, the Hindu tradition that phenomenal reality is the dream of Vishnu, asleep on the primal waters. We live inside his body and inside his dream (see Zimmer 1962, chap. 2).

Wendy Doniger O'Flaherty provides an enormous range of possibilities for the relationship between dream and waking in the Hindu tradition: that waking reality is as much a projection as a dream, that we are being dreamed by another, that the dream is the primary reality. Her *Dreams, Illusions, and Other Realities* reminds us that the commonsense Aristotelian observation that art is a secondary formation from nonart experience expresses a cultural and not an absolute judgement. Common sense is culturally bound (1984, introduction).

Our reluctance to seek absolute truth from either dreams or stories is a cultural change and is accompanied by a change in what determines common sense for us. In the West, at least, we have taken our dreams less seriously since we have ceased to live in a universe mythically arranged. Presumably the character of our dreams has altered to fit their new status. Certainly dreams alter according to what we think about them. When I teach Freud, I dream Freudian dreams; when I move to Jung, so do my dreams. I have run into similar observations many times. Behaviorists of my acquaintance do not recall dreams. Montague Ullman and his colleagues encountered telepathic dreams in their patients much less frequently when they ceased studying such dreams.

While literary traditions concerning dreams do not necessarily reflect exact observation, they do record what a culture expects of dreams. So do practices such as those connected with temples of Asklepios, as described by C. Kerenyi. Greeks suffering illnesses might go to such a temple for incubation. Following the performance of certain rituals, suppliants would go to sleep in expectation of a dream in which the god or his helper, Telesphoros, would either heal them directly or prescribe a remedy. From reports patients were not disappointed, at least not always.

We do not expect such direct healing from our dreams and do not petition gods for certain types of dreams. But we used to. The cessation of the oracles was certainly accompanied by a change in our narrative habits and might have signaled a change in our nocturnal narration as well. The move out of mythic consciousness was the single greatest change in our experiential world in the time of which we have records. Now we seem to be moving outside, or at least away from, plotted narratization.

Narrative Experience

Ironized narratives tend to disappear into stasis. Simple collocations of events without implied causality, as in some modern journalism, also undo narrative order. Such collocations are not ironic. They do not undo an otherwise implied causal system; they have no need to employ interruption or synchrony. Their basic technique is parataxis: simple addition, one fact after another until we know who, where, what, when, and how. If the story gets much into the *why* or invites us in that direction, it moves toward the kind of narration we have been discussing. The move toward objective journalism is a move away from narrative. The following wire story appeared on page A13 of the *New York Times* for 25 February 1985.

Poor Housekeeping is Given
As Reason for Wife's Murder

MASON, Mich., Feb. 24 (AP)—A man charged with shooting his wife to death told the police he was provoked by her poor cooking and sloppy housekeeping, officers said.

Stanley Diehl, 52 years old, said he had been upset about it for some time, Detective Richard Fitzgerald said at a preliminary hearing Thursday. Mr. Diehl was held for trial on a charge of second-degree murder in the death of his wife, Ellen, on Dec. 4.

The detective said he believed the couple's home had "not been properly cleaned in a year." It was filled with dust and cob-webs, and littered with dog manure and food, he said. The cleanest area was a bedroom where Mr. Diehl kept his rifles and shotguns, he said.

The story is closer to a full narrative than most news items. For example, it imputes a reason for the murder. However, it brackets naming the way meaning arises, and it is not concerned to undo an assumed mode of connection among events. We can imagine what Flannery O'Connor, or Chaucer, or Raymond Carver might have done with the news item. We have our own pity, anger, and wonder in reaction to the story. But unless we make a special effort, it does not become a narrative because it does not in its nature as journalism elicit a causal modality.

What Yurij Lotman calls *gossip* and sees, along with myth, as one of the sources of narrative, may be also one of its tendencies. Consider one of the shortest short stories in modern fiction, Richard Brautigan's "The Scarlatti Tilt" from *Revenge of the Lawn* (50, reproduced here in full).

"It's very hard to live in a studio apartment in San Jose with a man who's learning to play the violin." That's what she told the police when she handed them the empty revolver.

Stanley Fish, Norman Holland, and others have instructed us on how thoroughly involved we are as readers in eliciting meaning from a text. We do something with Brautigan's story that we do not do with the news item. Typographic and presentational cues help us engage the texts differently. "The Scarlatti Tilt," like every narrative, invites us to imagine a process occurring in a universe ruled by (or undone from) constraints on the possible and customary relationships among events. It invites us to accommodate something novel within conditions familiar to us from our literary experience. The news item does not ask to be integrated, merely noticed. "This thing happened." To move from "This thing happened" to "This is the sort of thing that happens in the world; the world is that way" is to move from gossip to narrative.

Narrative in its function of adapting us to change is inherently didactic. The distaste of the twentieth century for didactic literature amounts to a distaste for narrative.

Pointedly didactic literature does not typically acknowledge its real lesson. Brautigan's joke gives us a little model of how we might feel in a studio apartment, a little imaginatively implied experience in the midst of the humor. All he supplies is the aftermath. We know the life well enough to sense, without explicitly formulating, the rest of the plot. The filling-in movement of our mind comes effortlessly; it constitutes our narrative competence. The withholding of such movement is part of our competence as readers of newspapers.

As a short story, "The Scarlatti Tilt" is admirably polysemous. Did she shoot him or the violin? (We do know the composer of the piece he was playing when she fired.) When I first read the story I was quite sure that he was implied as her target, that she had killed him, and that he was her husband. That is, my reception of the text was firmly such, and I did not think of the violin as her target. Others saw it that way. I appealed to the atmosphere created by the presence of the police, his absence, and the expectation of homicidal violence in contemporary U.S. narrative. My adversaries (a sect of students) appealed to the greater subtlety, humor, and gentility of their reaction. They reacted in a richer dimension and had the superior experience. From that perspective, the story becomes a little character test that I fail.

Well, so be it. I see no way to resolve the difference nor any need to do so. Once I have grasped the other way that the text can mean, my informed experience of the text is improved. But what if I read the story as if I encountered it in a news item? I do not habitually interact with news items as I do short stories. I would read Brautigan's piece as deficient journalism. It has left me with too many curiosities. Given the intrinsic interest of the piece, I would probably violate my reading protocol and think about it a bit, treating it as a story. But taken as a newspaper piece, it ceases to engage my interest.

Narrative may be moving away from the Brautigan story and the response it evokes to the newspaper story and its protocol of response. Comic strips, sitcoms, and soaps all have a strong element of gossip. The irony of traditional soaps diminished in prime-time efforts such as "Mary Hartman, Mary Hartman" and "Soap," and the gossip element increased. In comic strips and sitcoms, the importance of the plot can become less prominent than the accumulation of simple incident as we see how characters will react to yet another situation. "The Cosby Show," a ratings favorite, has had only an episodic organization and not a full plot in the episodes I have seen. (I do not mean that it is somehow defective or to blame: I do mean that plot must not be that important to the current viewing audience.)

One effect of an increased consciousness of what narrative is and how it works is to disengage the reader emotionally from the text. Concerns about Western culture's apocalyptic proclivities may dissolve in our growing indifference to plot itself. I project a company of readers who will treat narratives more and more as gossip. A new interest in the unwitting self-revelations of the author or of the society that produced the text should accompany the shift in status of the narrative.

A change of the consciousness with which readers approach texts is a change in narrative itself, which depends on the set of author, text, world, and reader. The change may prove to be as great a watershed as the change from mythic to postmythic narration. Or maybe it just seems that important to me now, at the end of my book. I do see some further changes going on in my own relationship to narrative and in the literary community. They become major changes only by projection.

When I engage simple narratives now (most television fare, popular films and novels), I am often aware of the bones—the movement from one process stage to another. My engagement with more serious texts is tinged with anticipation of the analytical reflex that will come at the end, when I will try to understand the work in its proper context. If such disengagements were only the result of my work, and if I were the carrier of some mild and temporary infection, the effect would be of small importance. But I assume that insofar as I am doing anything significant, I am articulating what is occurring among readers in general. The change does not originate with anything you or I could choose to do, if it is real. From our efforts will originate only our understanding of the change. (A romantic argument, as the reader will have noticed.)

As we step further outside the imaginative realities of narrative we will probably worry still more about the relationships between narrative and nonnarrative experience, a shift now in progress. What does a given narrative do to the reader, if anything? How does a reader use it? Can an act of reading be value-free?

As for the writing of narrative, I suspect that we are closer to Orwell's novel-writing machines of *1984* than we were in 1948. I have written a book-length (unsold) romance since understanding what romance is and how it is built (insofar as I do; the reader has the evidence). I knew better what I had done once the stuff was written but still faced one blank page after another in the writing. A more detailed knowledge of plot structure did help me make broad plans, I believe. The writing of more simple narratives than my novel might be greatly eased by a consciousness of plot structure. Surely a greater sophistication as to the structure of sitcoms could streamline their production.

I anticipate that the change of consciousness regarding narrative will lead to a drop in its cultural prestige, which has in part been based on that whore, Mystery. Not that narrative itself is in danger of utterly disappearing, though it may diminish.

We must still accommodate the new within that which is familiar to us, and narrative seems to be our primary way to accomplish the task. The element of gossip may increase, but it is through narrative that those novel events enter the patterns of our lives. The effect of an increase in gossip is to weaken our location in time and space. I must say that I feel our culture is less firmly located than it was. I do not see this as all evil. Much better to act with a lesser degree of plottedness than to accept a plot of manifest destiny or the Armageddon plot. Literary feminism is very much concerned with the weakening of plot, which is often resented as if it were a colonially imposed structure. All of us are in for much more lyric exploration of the present as opposed to the drive of plot toward linearity and closure.

As linguistic consciousness seemed to call forth waking dreams, so a broadening of linguistic consciousness may lead to narrative employments I cannot foresee. In any case, we are unlikely to cease telling ourselves or one another stories. The kinds of stories we tell, and their status in our experience, however, do change.

We will change in ways I anticipate welcoming as a response to the shifting status of narrative. In my lifetime I am aware of a change in the ways I and, so far as I can tell, the culture in general receive narrative texts. Whatever changes await us will demand new efforts toward consciousness as we strive to understand the conditions of our existence. One set of those conditions promises to remain narrative and will reflect the shapes of human life—the shapes of narrative experience.

Works Cited

Aarne, Antti Amatus. 1961. *The Types of the Folktale: A Classification and Bibliography*. Translated and enlarged by Stith Thompson. 2d rev. Helsinki: Academica Scientarum Fennica.

Abrams, M. H. 1953. *The Mirror and the Lamp: Romantic Theory and the Critical Tradition*. New York: Oxford University Press.

Alcorn, Marshall W., Jr., and Mark Bracher. 1985. "Literature, Psychoanalysis, and the Re-Formation of the Self: A New Direction for Reader-Response Theory." *PMLA* 100:342–54.

"Backward Glance." 1985. In "Science and the Citizen." *Scientific American*, April, 82–83.

Baldwin, T. W. 1947. *Shakespeare's Five-Act Structure*. Urbana: University of Illinois Press.

Barratt, Barnaby B. 1984. *Psychic Reality and Psychoanalytic Knowing*. Vol. 3 of *Advances in Psychoanalysis: Theory, Research, and Practice*. Hillsdale, N.J.: The Psychoanalytic Press.

Barthes, Roland. 1974. *S/Z*. Translated from the French by Richard Miller. New York: Hill and Wang.

Bary, William Theodore de, Wing-tsit Chan, and Burton Watson, compilers. 1966. Vol. 1 of *Sources of Chinese Tradition*. New York: Columbia University Press.

Beckett, Samuel. 1954. *Waiting for Godot: Tragicomedy in Two Acts*. New York: Grove.

Bell, Andrea. 1986. "From Beyond the Limits of Expressibility: Samuel Beckett's *Waiting for Godot*." Unpublished essay.

Berne, Eric. 1964. *Games People Play: The Psychology of Human Relationships*. New York: Ballantine.

Blake, William. 1953. *Selected Poetry and Prose of William Blake*. Edited by Northrop Frye. New York: Random.

Breger, Louis. 1981. *Freud's Unfinished Journey: Conventional and Critical Perspectives in Psychoanalytic Theory*. London: Routledge.

Brooks, Peter. 1984. *Reading for the Plot: Design and Intention in Narrative*. New York: Knopf.

Campbell, Joseph. 1968. *The Hero with a Thousand Faces*. 2d ed. Bollingen Series 17. Princeton, N.J.: Princeton University Press.

Cohen, David B. 1979. *Sleep and Dreaming: Origins, Nature, and Functions*. New York: Pergamon.

Cohen, Ralph, ed. 1989. *The Future of Literary Theory*. New York: Routledge.

Crick, Francis, and Graeme Mitchison. 1983. "The Function of Dream Sleep." *Nature*, 14 July, 111–13.

Culler, Jonathan. 1975a. "Defining Narrative Units." In *Style and Structure in Literature: Essays in the New Stylistics*, edited by Roger Fowler, 123–42. Ithaca, N.Y.: Cornell University Press.

———. 1975b. *Structuralist Poetics*. Ithaca, N.Y.: Cornell University Press.

Cutts, John. 1968. "Shadow and Substance: Structural Unity in *Titus Andronicus*." *Comparative Drama* 2:161–72.

Danson, Lawrence. 1974. "The Device of Wonder: *Titus Andronicus* and Revenge Tragedies." *Texas Studies in Language and Literature* 16:27–43.

Derrida, Jacques. 1973. *Speech and Phenomena and Other Essays on Husserl's Theory of Signs*. Translated by David Allison. Evanston, Ill.: Northwestern University Press.

Dewald, Paul. 1972. *The Psychoanalytic Process: A Case Illustration*. NY: Basic.

Dewey, John. 1976. *Art as Experience*. New York: Norton.

Dundes, Alan, ed. 1983. *Cinderella: A Casebook*. New York: Wildman Press.

Dunlop, Charles E. M., ed. 1977. *Philosophical Essays on Dreaming*. Ithaca, N.Y.: Cornell University Press.

Eliade, Mircea. 1963. *Myth and Reality*. Translated by Willard R. Trask. World Perspectives Series 31. New York: Harper.

Felperin, Howard. 1972. *Shakespearean Romance*. Princeton, N.J.: Princeton University Press.

Fish, Stanley E. 1972. *Self-Consuming Artifacts: The Experience of Seventeenth-Century Literature*. Berkeley: University of California Press.

Fiss, Harry. 1979. "Kant Dream Research: A Psychobiological Perspective," In Wolman, op. cit., 20–75.

Fleming, W. H. 1902. *Shakespeare's Plots*. New York: Putnam.

Forster, E. M. 1927. *Aspects of the Novel*. New York: Harcourt.

Freud, Sigmund. 1953–74. *The Standard Edition of the Complete Psychological Works*. Translated and edited by James Strachey et al. 19 vols. London: Hogarth.

Frye, Northrop. 1969. *Anatomy of Criticism: Four Essays*. 1957; reprint, New York: Atheneum.

———. 1976. *The Secular Scripture: A Study of the Structure of Romance*. Cambridge: Harvard University Press.

————. 1965. "The Structure and Spirit of Comedy." In *Stratford Papers on Shakespeare*, edited by B. A. W. Jackson, 1–10. Toronto: Gage.

Fuller, Renee. 1982. "The Story as Engram: Is it Fundamental to Thinking?" *Journal of Mind and Behavior* 3, no. 2:127–42.

Gardiner, Muriel. 1971. *The Wolf-Man by the Wolf-Man, with The Case of the Wolf-Man, by Sigmund Freud and a Supplement by Ruth Mack Brunswick, Foreword by Anna Freud, Edited, with Notes, an Introduction, and Chapters by Muriel Gardiner.* New York: Basic.

Geertz, Clifford. 1973. *The Interpretation of Cultures: Selected Essays.* New York: Basic.

Goldsmith, Oliver. 1966. *Collected Works of Oliver Goldsmith.* Vol. 5. Edited by Arthur Friedman. London: Oxford University Press.

Gombrich, E. H. 1961. *Art and Illusion: A Study in the Psychology of Pictorial Representation.* Bollingen Series, vol. 35, no. 5. 2d ed. Princeton: Princeton University Press.

Grimm, Jacob and Wilhelm. 1966. *Kinder-und Hausmarchen, gesammelt durch die Bruder Grimm, Zeichnungen und Farbige Blatter von Gerhard Oberlander.* 4th ed. Munich: H. Ellermann.

Grogan, Emmett. 1972. *Ringolevio: A Life Played for Keeps.* Boston: Little, Brown.

Guillen, Claudio. 1971. *Literature as System: Essays Toward the Theory of Literary History.* Princeton, N.J.: Princeton University Press.

Halsband, Robert. 1966. "Speaking of Books: Oliver Goldsmith." *New York Times Book Review*, 30 Oct., 64.

Hamilton, A. C. 1963. "*Titus Andronicus*: The Form of Shakespearian Tragedy." *Shakespeare Quarterly* 14:201–13.

Haskell, Robert E., ed. 1986. *Cognition and Dream Research.* Special issue, *Journal of Mind and Behavior* 7, nos. 2 and 3 (Spring and Summer):1–331.

Himmelfarb, Gertrude. 1984. "Denigrating the Rule of Reason: The 'New History' Goes Bottom-Up." *Harper's*, April, 84–90.

Holland, Norman N. 1985. *The I.* New Haven, Conn.: Yale University Press.

Hunt, Harry. 1989. *The Multiplicity of Dreams: Imagination and Consciousness.* New Haven, Conn.: Yale University Press.

Jakobson, Roman. 1987. *Language in Literature.* Edited by Krystyna Pomorska and Stephen Rudy. Cambridge: Harvard University Press.

Jaynes, Julian. 1976. *The Origin of Consciousness in the Breakdown of the Bicameral Mind.* Boston: Houghton.

Jenkins, Harold. 1955. "*As You Like It.*" *Shakespeare Survey* 8:40–51.

Jones, Emrys. 1971. *Scenic Form in Shakespeare.* New York: Oxford University Press.

Jones, Ernest. 1976. *Hamlet and Oedipus.* New York: Norton.

Jung, Carl G. 1970. *The Collected Works of Carl G. Jung*. Edited by G. Adler et al. Translated by R.F.C. Hull. 2d ed. 20 vols. Bollingen Series 20. Princeton, N.J.: Princeton University Press.

Kerenyi, C. 1959. *Asklepios: Archetypal Image of the Physician's Existence*. Translated by Ralph Manheim. Bollingen Series 65.3. New York: Pantheon.

Kermode, Frank. 1967. *The Sense of an Ending: Studies in the Theory of Fiction*. London: Oxford University Press.

Levinson, Daniel J., with Charlotte N. Darrow, Edward B. Klein, and Braxton McKee. 1978. *The Seasons of a Man's Life*. New York: Knopf.

Lévi-Strauss, Claude. 1967. *Structural Anthropology*. Translated by Claire Jacobson and Brooke Grundfest Schoepf. Garden City, N.Y.: Anchor Books.

Lotman, Jurij M. 1979. "The Origin of Plot in the Light of Typology." *Poetics Today* 1, nos. 1 and 2:161–84.

Lukács, Georg. 1971. *The Theory of the Novel: A Historico-Philosophical Essay on the Forms of Great Epic Literature*. Translated by Anna Bostock. 1920; reprint, Cambridge: MIT Press.

Malcolm, Norman. 1959. *Dreaming*. London: Routledge.

Masson, Jeffrey Moussaieff. 1984. *The Assault on Truth: Freud's Suppression of the Seduction Theory*. New York: Farrar.

Mercier, Vivian. 1956. "The Uneventful Event," *Irish Times*, 18 February.

Mincoff, Marco. 1965. "Shakespeare's Comedies and the Five-Act Structure." *Bulletin de la Faculté des Lettres de Strasbourg* 63, no. 8:919–34.

Natterson, Joseph M., ed. 1980. *The Dream in Clinical Practice*. New York: Aronson.

Neumann, Erich. 1954. *The Origin and History of Consciousness*. Foreword by C.G. Jung. Translated by R.F.C. Hull. Bollingen Series 42. Princeton, N.J.: Princeton University Press.

Nevo, Ruth. 1972. *Tragic Form in Shakespeare*. Princeton, N.J.: Princeton University Press.

Nishida, Kitaro. 1990. *An Enquiry into the Good*. Translated by Masao Abe and Christopher Ives. New Haven, Conn.: Yale University Press.

Obholzer, Karen. 1982. *The Wolf-Man: Conversations with Freud's Patient—Sixty Years Later*. Translated by Michael Shaw. New York: Continuum.

O'Flaherty, Wendy Doniger. 1984. *Dreams, Illusions, and Other Realities*. Chicago: University of Chicago Press.

Palmer, D. J. 1972. "The Unspeakable in Pursuit of the Uneatable: Language and Action in *Titus Andronicus*." *Critical Quarterly* 14 :320–39.

Palombo, Stanley R. 1984. "Recovery of Early Memories Associated with Reported Dream Imagery." *American Journal of Psychiatry* 141:1508–11.

Paris, Bernard. 1974. *A Psychological Approach to Fiction*. Bloomington: Indiana University Press.

Peterson, Douglas L. 1973. *Time, Tide, and Tempest: A Study of Shakespeare's Romances*. San Marino, Calif.: Huntington Library.

Pettet, E. C. 1970. *Shakespeare and the Romance Tradition*. London: Methuen.

Phillips, Mark. 1983–84. "The Revival of Narrative: Thoughts on a Current Historiographical Debate." *University of Toronto Quarterly* 53, no. 2 (Winter):149–65.

Price, Hereward T. 1943. "The Authorship of *Titus Andronicus*." *Journal of English and Germanic Philology* 42:55–81.

Priest, John F. 1970. "Myth and Dream in Hebrew Scripture." In *Myths, Dreams, and Religion*, edited by Joseph Campbell, 48–67. New York: Dutton.

Propp, Vladimir. 1968. *Morphology of the Folktale*. Translated by Laurence Scott. 2d ed., edited by Louis A. Wagner. Austin: University of Texas Press.

Radin, Paul. 1972. *The Trickster: A Study in American Indian Mythology*. With commentaries by Karl Kerenyi and C.G. Jung. New York: Schocken.

Reese, Jack E. 1970. "The Formalization of Horror in *Titus Andronicus*." *Shakespeare Quarterly* 21:77–84.

Ricoeur, Paul. 1984–88. *Time and Narrative*. Vols. 1 and 2. translated by Kathleen McLaughlin and David Pellauer; vol. 3 translated by Kathleen Blamey and David Pellauer. Chicago: University of Chicago Press.

Schafer, Roy. 1976. *A New Language for Psychoanalysis*. New Haven, Conn.: Yale University Press.

Sells, Arthur Lytton. 1974. *Oliver Goldsmith: His Life and Works*. New York: Barnes.

Shakespeare, William. 1968. *As You Like It*. Edited by H. J. Oliver. Harmondsworth: Penguin.

Snuggs, Henry L. 1960. *Shakespeare and Five Acts: Studies in a Dramatic Convention*. New York: Vantage.

Snyder, F. 1966. "Toward an Evolutionary Theory of Dreaming." *American Journal of Psychiatry* 123:121–36.

Spence, Donald P. 1982. *Narrative Truth and Historical Truth: Meaning and Interpretation in Psychoanalysis*. New York: Norton.

Sulloway, Frank J. 1979. *Freud, Biologist of the Mind: Beyond the Psychoanalytic Legend*. New York: Basic.

Teilhard de Chardin. 1965. *The Phenomenon of Man*. Translated by Bernard Wall. 2d ed. New York: Harper.

Tilley, Allen. 1978a. "The Counterculture Trickster." *Psychocultural Review* 2, no. 1 (Winter):54–61.

————. 1978b. "The Modes of Fiction: A Plot Morphology." *College English* 39, no. 6 (February):692–706.

Tobias, Richard C., and Paul G. Zolbrod, eds. 1974. *Shakespeare's Late Plays: Essays in Honor of Charles Crow*. Athens: Ohio University Press.

Todorov, Tzvetan. 1975. *The Fantastic: A Structural Approach to a Literary Genre*. Translated from the French by Richard Howard. Ithaca: Cornell University Press.

Tolkien, J.R.R. 1966. "On Fairy Tales" in *The Tolkien Reader*. New York: Ballantine.

Udwin, Victor. 1987. "Reading the Red Ball: A Phenomenology of Literary Process." In *Narrative Poetics: Innovations, Limits, Challenges*, edited by James Phelan, 115–26. Columbus: Center for Comparative Studies in Humanities, Ohio State University Press.

Ullman, Montague, Stanley Krippner, and Alan Vaughan. 1973. *Dream Telepathy*. NY: Macmillan, 1973.

Ungerer, Gustav. 1961. "An Unrecorded Elizabethan Performance of *Titus Andronicus*." *Shakespeare Survey* 14:102–9.

Volkan, Vamik D. 1984. *What Do You Get When You Cross a Dandelion with a Rose? The True Story of a Psychoanalysis*. New York: Jason Aronson.

Waith, Eugene. 1957. "The Metamorphosis of Violence in *Titus Andronicus*." *Shakespeare Survey* 10:39–49.

————, ed. 1984. *Titus Andronicus*. The Oxford Shakespeare Edition. London: Oxford University Press.

Wimsatt, William K. 1954. *The Verbal Icon: Studies in the Meaning of Poetry*. Lexington: University of Kentucky Press.

Winget, Carolyn N., and Milton Kramer. 1970. *Dimensions of Dreams*. Gainesville: University of Florida Press.

Wolman, Benjamin B., ed. 1979. *Handbook of Dreams: Research, Theories and Applications*. New York: Van Nostrand Reinhold.

Young, David. 1972. *The Heart's Forest: A Study of Shakespeare's Pastoral Plays*. New Haven, Conn.: Yale University Press.

Zimmer, Heinrich. 1962. *Myths and Symbols in Indian Art and Civilization*. Edited by Joseph Campbell. Bollingen Series 6. New York: Harper.

Index

Library of Congress Cataloging-in-Publication Data

Tilley, Allen.
    Plot snakes and the dynamics of narrative experience / Allen
Tilley.
        p.   cm.
    Includes bibliographical references and index.
    ISBN 0–8130–1151–5 (alk. paper)
    1. Narration (Rhetoric)   2. Plots (Drama, novels, etc.)
I. Title.
PN212.T5   1992   92–5428
808—dc20   CIP